SOUL CARE
—— FOR ——
CAREGIVERS

*How to Help Yourself
While Helping Others*

Susanne West

Human Sun Media
Sonoma, California

Human
Sun
Media

ISBN: 1466434694
ISBN-13: 9781466434691

To Heidi – You inspire me every day

Table of Contents

Introduction

"Needs? What needs? I don't have time to even think about my needs." This is the theme song of the typical caregiver. Whether a professional caregiver or a family member who is providing care for someone who is ill or disabled, caregivers are stressed and overworked. Many of you are exhausted, depleted, and overwhelmed. The American Medical Association identifies caregivers as the "hidden patients." As caregivers, you need help, too.

Tending to your own needs may seem to be impossible if you are one of these very busy caregivers. You probably relegate self-care to the bottom of your "to-do" list, assuming it's there at all. After all, you're the strong one, the dependable one, not the one with needs. As a result of working with caregivers, and from many years of personal experience as a caregiver, I've come to believe that self-care is anything but optional. It is imperative.

This book is for you, the caregiver. There are many of you, and your numbers are growing every day. According to the National Alliance for Caregiving, in 2011, 65.7 million people in the U.S. provided some type of care to a friend or relative with a life-altering illness. In 2004, this figure was 44 million. Of these, more than one-half provided ongoing care beyond one year, with the average length of time being 4.6 years.

Health care is the second fastest growing sector of the U.S. economy, employing over ten million workers. Besides these paid caregivers, there are countless volunteers: friends, neighbors, and family members. Caregiving has become big business, and there is no indication of a decrease in the future.

Caregiving for people with life-altering illnesses, in even the best of circumstances, can be stressful. It is fraught with challenges. Yet, providing care to someone in need can also be the most rewarding work you will ever do. Caregiving is soul work. Just as illness can be a life-changing experience, so too can caregiving be, presenting you with opportunities to learn and grow. Caregiving can change you in profound ways. In *Soul Care for Caregivers: How to Help Yourself While Helping Others,* you will find tools, information, suggestions, personal anecdotes, and insights from caregivers. These are intended to help you care for your soul while caring for others.

My Caregiving Journey

I've been a caregiver for most of my life. By age four, I was doctor, nurse, and teacher to all of my dolls and stuffed animals. Consumed by this passion, I sectioned off a third of my bedroom to create a combination hospital, doctor's office, and classroom. My mother tells me that, at age three, I bandaged the eyes of all of my dolls, bears, and plush bunnies and then gave them pink, white, and yellow candy pills. "You went through a doctor kit every six months," she tells me. "And you had that stethoscope around your neck most of the time, always checking our hearts and seeing if we needed shots." Dr. Moss, my pediatrician, gave me a "little something" each time I was at his office: a tongue depressor or a few cotton swabs. These priceless possessions lit me up. I had no interest in lolli-pops. I just wanted the doctor stuff.

When I wasn't ministering to sick patients and my family, I was teaching. When the children were healthy enough to be released from the hospital, they returned to school and sat dutifully in rows in my makeshift classroom where I taught them reading, writing, and arithmetic, and read them many stories. Inevitably, they'd become ill again with colds, sore throats, measles, and chickenpox, or they would fall from the monkey bars and break an arm or a leg. Then it was back to my hospital for them. When I was old enough to read books, my heroes were Nurse Cherry Ames from the popular children's book series, Clara Barton, and Albert Schweitzer. Above all others, I revered Florence Nightingale.

At eleven, I was the neighborhood therapist to whom kids brought their problems and secrets. I was on call 24/7, available for listening and giving advice whenever someone needed me. In addition, I signed up to be a candy-striper in a local hospital and was elated to come home after school, put on my nurse-like apron, go into real hospital rooms with real equipment, and be with real patients. I was in heaven.

At fifteen, I found myself in a caregiving role with my fourteen-year-old brother who had been recently diag-nosed with paranoid schizophrenia. For much of his life, until he died at age 36, I was very involved with him, help-ing to meet his needs, and always on the lookout for meth-ods of helping him. There were times when I was the only family member with whom he would communicate. He called me his "rock." Observing my brother's intense suf-fering was a heartbreaking experience for all of us. The many years of emotional support and searching for the right care and treatments for him took a great toll on our whole family.

Scott was a kind and gentle soul, and I cared deeply about him. He was quite lucid most of the time and able to clearly articulate his torment and nightmarish inner world. He experienced little relief from the myriad treatments he received, and I had never felt so helpless and hopeless. At times, it was close to unbearable for me to see my dear, sweet brother in psychiatric treatment facilities and half-way houses, often in despair or fear, sometimes hauntingly silent. It seemed as if he was trapped in his mind and body, urgently and desperately aching to be released.

It was also painful to witness the great suffering of other young men and women with mental illness. I was often scared by what I saw, but hid my fear. I wanted to be the strong one for Scott and also didn't want my parents to see how frightened I was and that this was tearing me apart. I thought that they already had too much to bear. I suffered silently and felt very alone.

As arduous as serving Scott was, it changed our family in ways that nothing else could have. Our caregiving opened our hearts, strengthened us as individuals and as a family, and helped us to discover what really matters in life. We became more humane, compassionate, and sensitive. My natural inclination towards being a caregiver, along with my experiences with Scott, motivated me to have a career in the helping professions. I became a life coach, integrative spiritual teacher, lecturer, group facilitator, and psychology professor, all work that I continue to do.

In 1982, when Scott was thirty-six, he committed suicide. The shock, searing pain, and grief of that loss dropped me into very deep and dark places in my psyche. I was undone by this, as were my parents and our entire family. We reflected back on the years of Scott's suffering and the anguish we all endured. In addition to that tragic event having a wrenching impact on me, it also strengthened my desire to help alleviate suffering in others.

It so happened that I had entered a counseling psychology program the same month as Scott's death. The first year of that program was grueling for me because I was in so much distress. I was in the perfect school, though, to explore and work through my emotional pain. The program focused on personal growth and development and had a strong experiential component. There was an understanding that to be an effective counselor you needed to be keenly self-aware and ever-willing to identify and confront your unresolved psychological material. In class after class, we read, talked, and, it seemed, endlessly unearthed and processed the unhealed wounds in our psyches. As part of the program, we had to be in therapy. It turned out to be the most ideal environment I could have been in to receive help and support in moving through this very painful phase of my life.

In addition to all of the personal healing and revelations, I received wonderful instruction and guidance regarding how to be an effective helper for others. Throughout my graduate course of study and to this day, I have explored many questions: What causes psychological distress and mental illness? What heals? What impedes healing? What constitutes healthy caregiving? Why are some people more resilient than others? How can we foster resilience? What are the links between spirituality and healing?

Seven years later, in 1989, my daughter, Heidi, then eighteen, was diagnosed with Ankylosing Spondylitis and Crohn's disease. Ankylosing Spondylitis (A.S.) is a chronic, degenerative form of arthritis, primarily affecting the spine and sacroiliac joints, eventually causing fusion of the spine. Crohn's disease is an inflammatory bowel disease. At this time, there are no known cures for these conditions. When I became a mother, my worst fear had been that something awful, either physically or emotionally, would happen to my daughter. I thought that I could survive any other life challenge. I was convinced that this type of misfortune was a life experience I could never handle. I had watched my parents stretched to the edge of their capacity for over twenty years, loving and caring for a son who was mentally ill and then, after his suicide, my mother barely able to stay alive herself.

My life was turned upside down with the onset of Heidi's debilitating illnesses. However, my experience as a primary caregiver greatly accelerated my psychological and spiritual growth. The experience was, and continues to be, a powerful catalyst for transformation in my life. Every area of my life—finances, health, work, relationships, and family—has been affected by this experience. In addition to my own personal growth and transformation, it became both a necessity and an opportunity to learn everything I could about healthy caregiving. For example, I learned more about the importance of self-care and emotional and spiritual renewal, the difference between empathy and sympathy, rescuing vs. healthy helping, boundaries and limit-setting, the importance of support, and issues related to caregiver stress and "compassion fatigue."

As a result of my personal experiences with caregiving and from working with many formal and informal caregivers in my private practice, community organizations, and university classes, I developed Soul Care for Caregivers workshops for professional and family caregivers. Initially, these programs were offered to professional cancer caregivers, that is, physicians, nurses, nurses' aides, social workers, psychotherapists, and other health care practitioners. I had received a grant from The Lloyd Symington Foundation, which funds grassroots creative programs for the cancer community. Some of these formal caregivers were also family caregivers. I quickly discovered that the content and exercises I'd created were equally applicable to both groups and decided to open the workshops to all types of caregivers.

Honoring Your Own Needs

You are more likely to maintain a high quality of care for the people you serve and be able to reap the profound rewards that come from serving others if you are able to identify and honor your own needs. I believe that it's possible to reduce many of the stressors associated with caregiving if you receive support and learn tools and strategies for accessing your rich inner resources, such as creativity and intuition. An important aspect of Soul Care for Caregivers work is to provide opportunities for you to explore the spiritual dimensions of your experience through personal writing, self-guided imagery, and other creative processes, asking questions, such as:

- What is the deeper meaning of this experience in my life?
- What qualities am I developing as a result of this experience?
- What am I learning?
- How am I growing?

I have personally experienced, and witnessed in many others, the potential for caregiving to be a deeply trans-formational journey.

Many caregivers are resistant to focusing on self-care. You feel you don't have enough time and energy to focus on yourself. You think you should be strong and capable at all times and shouldn't have personal needs. You see looking after yourself as avoiding responsibilities. You imagine you will be perceived as selfish or weak if you take time to care for yourself. You envision something terrible happening to your care receiver if you're not focused on them and their care at all times. Yet, if you aren't aware of your own needs and willing to allow time and energy for self-care, you suffer and so does your caregiving.

In the difficult months preceding my daughter's diagnoses and for about a year after, I was consumed with caring for her. I was obsessed with doing everything humanly possible on all practical fronts and with providing emotional and moral support for Heidi, as well. Whenever I had free time, I'd feel guilty if I didn't use that time for doing more research about her conditions, investigating treatments, or looking for books or tapes she'd enjoy. Throughout, I was highly stressed because of the severity of her symptoms, the pain she was experiencing, and the complications around finding the right treatments and practitioners. Getting entangled in the health care maze and dealing with insurance was another huge stressor.

A wonderful friend, Toni, took me to lunch and firmly told me that she could no longer sit by and watch me "run myself into the ground." She pointed out that I was not seeing how overwhelmed I was and that she could see it was beginning to impact the quality of my caregiving. "Susanne," she said, "you must take care of yourself. It's not an option. If you can't do this for yourself, do it for Heidi. She needs you to be whole and complete, and you're not."

That was the day I made the choice to direct the helping toward myself. I started meditating and exercising again. I went to a few movies and picked up my pens and magazines to resume drawing and making collages. I became revitalized. In a few months, I regained my life force, and dare I say, I learned that it was possible to feel good and have fun even though my daughter was still hurting. I learned how to delegate and enlist help from others for Heidi's care and discovered that things moved along just fine—perhaps better—without my 24/7 presence.

I have now become quite an expert at balancing self-care with care for Heidi and the grandchildren. Heidi has three children, aged two, four, and six. The youngest, Sadie, has Down syndrome. The temptation is often great to give up me to spend more time helping out with all of the children, conducting research on Down syndrome, networking with colleagues and practitioners for children with special needs, and contributing financially for Sadie's care and well-being. I listen carefully all the time now, checking in with myself to make sure that I am able and want to help at any given time and that my help is truly needed. I no longer automatically jump in to "save the day." I am ever aware of the potential costs—to me, to Heidi, and to the rest of the family—of giving myself away.

This is, of course, not always an easy matter, and I make plenty of mistakes. There is a fine line between too much and too little helping, with no hard and fast rules. No longer a perfectionist, though, I don't spend time making myself wrong for being a fallible human. We teach what we need to learn.

Soul Care for Caregivers—What You'll Find Inside

Chapter One—Soul Gifts: The Rewards of Caregiving explores how you can find meaning, gifts, and opportunities for growth from difficult caregiving experiences. This chapter provides creative exercises to help you discover your "soul gifts."

Chapter Two—Boulders on the Path: The Stressors of Caregiving examines the challenges that caregivers experience, including work overload, time pressure, physical and emotional demands, and lack of or unreliable support. Guidelines for managing your stress and self-guided imagery practices are presented in this chapter.

Chapter Three—Where You End and I Begin: Boundaries discusses personal boundaries and limit-setting. You will learn how healthy boundaries contribute to healthy caring and receive techniques for developing good boundaries.

Chapter Four—Creativity is Good Medicine: Creativity for the Caregiver looks at the links between creativity and well-being in the context of caregiving and shows you how creative expression can be healing to your body, mind, emotions, and spirit. You are offered writing exercises, a creativity self-assessment, and a self-guided imagery process—all tools that will help you tap into your creative spirit.

Chapter Five—The Voice of Your Soul: Intuition and Caregiving demonstrates how having a strong connection to intuition can benefit all aspects of your caregiving experience. This chapter contains numerous techniques to help you tap into intuitive knowing. You will learn how to apply intuition to decision-making and to the challenges you encounter in caregiving.

Chapter Six—The Write Way to Well-Being: How to Create a Caregiver's Journal explores journaling as a tool for healing and transformation for you as caregivers. This chapter offers you guidelines for creating a Caregiver's Journal, with many specific ideas and journaling techniques.

Chapter Seven—Caregivers Speak: Stories and Wisdom from Caregivers is comprised of interviews that I conducted with four family caregivers and four caregiving professionals about their personal experiences and lessons learned from caregiving.

Chapter Eight—Practicing What I Teach presents some of my final thoughts and an account of two personal experiences with caregiving that transpired during the writing of this book.

Appendix One provides additional guidelines and practical suggestions for building your resilience and enhancing well-being.

Appendix Two explores self-criticism and its impact on your caregiving. You will learn how to tame the "Inner Critic."

Appendix Three provides website resources for caregiver information and support.

How to Use This Book

Soul Care for Caregivers: How to Help Yourself While Helping Others contains a variety of writing exercises and self-guided imagery processes. I wanted this book to do more than provide you with information. The exercises are designed to be transformative, to give you hands-on techniques to tap into your intuition, develop your strengths, manage stress, and access your creativity.

Like my workshops, this book provides you with optional, experiential activities that can enhance your well-being, further your personal growth, and help you develop resilience in your caregiving. These are tools that you can use again and again. You may also want to share some of the processes with your care recipient(s) as tools for their healing and transformation.

You can do the exercises when you come to them, or you may choose to do them at another time. The book doesn't have to be read cover to cover. Dip into the different sections as you're drawn to them. For example, if you are experiencing stress, you may want to begin with *Chapter Two—Boulders on the Path: The Stressors of Caregiving* and come back to *Chapter One—Soul Gifts: The Rewards of Caregiving* at another time. Follow your natural inclinations, and work with the book in any way that feels right to you.

When you work with the exercises, I recommend that you relax and center yourself for a few minutes before you

13

begin. For the self-guided meditations, you can memorize the essentials, record them, or have someone read them aloud to you. Experiment to see what works best for you.

Choose the exercises that appeal to you. Repeat them as often as you desire. Work at your own pace. You may want to spend some time each day, for example, focusing on intuitive or creative development. Perhaps creating a Caregiver's Journal is your focus for a while. Feel free to tailor the exercises to suit your own needs and work with those that are most relevant to you at a particular time. Make the processes your own.

Chapter 1

SOUL GIFTS: THE REWARDS OF CAREGIVING

I can't let Heidi keep lying on the floor of this hotel bathroom. She's whiter than the tile—that ghostly pale she gets when she's in a Crohn's flare-up. And she's got to be freezing. It's the coldest night in six years in Boston. I have to get my daughter up off that floor. But she wants me to stay back, be quiet. The word "helpless" barely touches what I feel. My kid is curled up in a ball three feet from me, her gut in flames, sharp pain repeatedly stabbing her abdomen again and again, hardly any time at all between the jolts of pain. And I can do nothing.

It goes on for hours—cramping and twisting, soft moans, loud groans, deep sighs. Do the sighs signal breaks in the waves of pain? I don't know, and Heidi can't tell me. She's caught in the jaws of suffering. It's like the worst stage of labor, but at least with labor you know there's a baby on the other side. This is nothing but bad news.

Lying next to her on the floor and, then finally, beside her on the bed, I'm overwhelmed. I feel that I can't bear watching her suffer for even one more second. This image from the night before in our hotel room keeps flashing in my mind as we board the plane from Boston to San Francisco in 1992. Heidi is teetering beside me, holding onto every available handrail to keep herself from falling. Half of me is in Dutiful Mom mode—responsible and efficient, getting the job done, moving us from the hotel to the airporter bus to the boarding gate. The other half of me is anxiously tracking her every move, every breath. Once on the plane, Heidi collapses into the seat, damp strands of her long blond hair falling across her eyes. She is shivering. I wrap my coat around her and add a blanket from the overhead bin. But it doesn't help. She continues to shiver until she finally drops off to sleep, exhausted.

As I watch her sleep, I reflect on the irony of the situation. Here I am, on the way back from a conference where we've deeply immersed ourselves in Buddhist teachings, and it's dawning on me that I've learned more from Heidi's illnesses over the past four years than from two decades of spiritual practice and study. A list starts to form in my mind of qualities that I've been inadvertently developing since the onset of her symptoms: presence, empathy, courage, strength, acceptance, resilience, generosity, trust, mindfulness, and compassion. I realize that this is what spiritual practice is all about.

Is it possible, I wonder, that her diseases really are blessings in my life, catalyzing transformation in ways I never could have imagined? I see that just about everything about me has changed over the last few years—my understanding of what's really important in life, beliefs about who I am and what I can and cannot do, old patterns, illusions, coping strategies, ways of being in the world and with others, and beliefs about health and healing, life, death, and suffering. I see that the events of the last four years have put me on a spiritual fast track.

I pull out my journal and write for more than two hours, feeling like a speeding train is moving through me. I'm flooded with insights. I can barely keep up. I see how important last night has been for my development—a situation I've dreaded has actually come about; I'm alone with Heidi during a serious flare-up in a place far away from our family, our friends, and her doctors. Filling page after page, I begin to see that something like this has happened before, when Heidi first called to tell me that she thought she had a "bad disease." These events and many others, I now start to understand, have been my Mt. Everest, my heroine's journey. And not only have I survived these soul tests, I've grown from them, in all the ways I had hoped to grow before any of these circumstances entered my life.

The phrase "gifts of an illness" occurs to me, and I write it down. I decide to begin chronicling the ways in which my experience of Heidi's illnesses is transforming me. And as this new resolution takes hold, my perspective begins to shift. Self-pity gives way to a deep, quiet sense that all these events and circumstances hold a meaning and that it's infinitely larger than I had ever supposed.

Discovering the Rewards

We try to set up our lives to avoid pain, discomfort, and unpredictability. Caregiving tosses all of that out the window. Here we are—sometimes very suddenly—in an intimate encounter with all that we have feared and hoped we'd never have to face: illness, pain, and suffering. We want to run and hide, to fix it, to change it, to make it go away. Caregiving is deep soul work. It's the soul work that takes place in the trenches, not on the mountaintop or in the meditation hall.

Illness is life changing; so is caregiving. It's a curse, and it's also a gift. Very little is spared on this transformational journey. Here's what is impacted in your caregiving experience: your finances, health, time for self and for others, emotions, spirituality, values, priorities, relationships, worldview, sanity, peace of mind, sense of control, daily routines, sleep, diet, work, and energy.

Caregiving takes us outside and often way beyond our comfort zones. The physical, mental, and emotional demands stretch us. We find ourselves in situations we may have dreaded for much of our lives. But then, isn't this where real growth is—beyond the known, the comfortable, the familiar? Our personalities recoil at the thought of this. Our souls, though, want us to shed old habits at all costs, even if it means being uncomfortable and entering dangerous territory. Perhaps, our souls are viewing this as the opportunity of a lifetime. Spiritual questions arise in the course of our caregiving: What is the meaning of life? What is death? What is important when we're alive? What is the place of suffering, pain, and illness? Why are we here? What can we control? What is beyond our control? Why them, and not me?

Caregivers are either in or have been in or will be in the most trying of life's circumstances. Some of you look worn-out, ragged, strained; others are hearty or bright-eyed. Overall, there is a depth that can be sensed in you, seen in your eyes, heard in your voices. One of the things I love about working with caregivers is that you are so soulful. You don't coast on small talk or superficial concerns. I love this about you. We are kindred spirits, part of a fast-growing club whose members are walking bravely into the dark night and changing at our cores. We have lost our innocence, but gained a depth and strength that has brought us closer to our true essence.

In my workshops, there is a section called *The Gifts of Caregiving*, in which caregivers share the personal rewards of their experiences, including how they are changing or what they are learning about themselves and life.

Greg said, "I've been a selfish person for so much of my life, and my wife and brothers would agree. Having to be there now so completely for my brother Jack, who has a very painful bone cancer, has changed me. I actually feel better than I have my entire life, and I know it's because I'm putting someone besides me first. It's all so strange. Here's this awful situation—believe me I feel horrible about it, especially with all the pain he's in, and I feel more fulfilled than ever before."

June commented: "Louise never let me in before her illness. We've been distant since we were kids. I was jealous of all the attention she got from our dad because she was so pretty and so smart. I felt invisible, and I resented the heck out of her for it. Now, it's as if all of that never happened. I love her to pieces. We've had long cries about what we've both missed out on. As terrible as this sounds, I don't think this coming together would have happened were it not for her having breast cancer."

Paula spoke up next. "I found out how capable and strong I am. That's certainly not how I saw myself before. Somehow, I've managed to keep my job at the phone company. I'm doing pretty well there. Along with balancing my work responsibilities, I've managed to be my mother's caregiver. I've become quite the skillful juggler. I even manage to find time to get in a trip to the gym every now and then. I've learned to ask for help, and some of my friends are pitching in, but I'm doing a lot myself. I didn't know I had it in me."

Manuel, a hospice nurse, shared that he often felt uplifted on his shifts. "Of course, you witness every sad thing you can imagine, but the expressions of gratitude that I receive from these courageous people and from their families and friends, simply make my day."

An emergency room nurse, Sara, said: "The hours are long. We're understaffed, overworked, and underpaid. But I wouldn't give up my job for anything. Words can't describe how I feel when I know that someone's health is improving or a patient has less fear because of the care I've extended to him or her. Giving of myself, in even small ways, to family members who are worried, afraid, and feeling helpless, is utterly gratifying. I know I'm making a difference in people's lives where there's great pain and suffering. This gives my life meaning. I feel like I'm fulfilling my life's purpose."

At the beginning of *The Gifts of Caregiving* section of the workshop, some participants, especially those that are right in the middle of a particularly difficult time, are understandably unable to see anything but the challenges they're confronting. Some of them purse their lips or cross their arms and legs. They cannot relate to the idea that there could possibly be anything good about this nightmare they are immersed in. Then, they hear Greg, June, Manuel, and others, and I can practically see light bulbs coming on all over the room.

"I guess I am a more open-hearted man since my father's stroke," said Jerry. "I do cry. Actually, I cry a lot. I guess that's a good thing for a guy who's always been the tough one. I was always so proud that I never let anything get to me." He wipes a tear from his eye.

"My values have changed," says Noreen, whose youngest daughter has leukemia. "My hair, my nails and clothes, and how gorgeous my house looked counted for so much. This experience with Sherry has turned me inside out. I was one shallow person. No more. I barely glance at myself in the mirror these days, and I haven't been to the hairdresser for weeks. I can see how superficial all that really was."

Christopher shared that he and Will have been best friends since high school. "We've been through his two marriages, my one, our kids, successes, and failures. We've been through it all together. We've lived in different parts of the county and even lost touch a few times. He's like a brother. Two years ago, when my dad died, he showed up for me like no one else did. Now, it's my turn to do that for him. He's one of the most generous people I've ever known. I can see that this help I'm giving him now is a way I'm able to give back a small amount of the care he's so generously bestowed on me."

Discovering the hidden treasures in our caregiving experiences can greatly shift our perspective about this often harrowing ordeal. Upon reflection, we discover that caregiving truly is a soul event. It is an initiation of sorts, a passage into new realms of experience and growth. We mature; we change; we discover inner resources we had no idea were available to us. We shed old skins and, often, discover a tender, loving soul beneath the crust of our conditioning. We gain access to feelings that have been buried for years and to a capacity for selflessness that we thought only the Mother Teresas of the world could exhibit. We become more real. We know how to yearn, to agonize, to love, to cry, to reach out, to survive our own mistakes and imperfections, to have conversations we never thought possible. We learn how to stand tall in the face of hardship and pain, and then, we learn how to pick ourselves up and begin again.

I had met and known parents whose children had died or been the victims of terrible mental and physical illnesses and was sure I could never endure what they did. When a friend of mine told me that her mother "went to bed for three years when her son was diagnosed with multiple sclerosis," I understood completely and remember thinking, "I'd do the same thing." Rising to meet the impossible and finding myself becoming as strong, capable, and often selfless as I'd seen others become was quite the revelation.

These opportunities for growth have become a regular part of my life. If you had told me two years ago that I'd be the very proud grandma of a baby with Down syndrome and that I'd feel like giving a huge hug to every child, man, and woman I see on the streets who has any kind of physical or mental disability, I'd say you were crazy. I was never able to connect wholeheartedly with people with visible disabilities unless I knew them personally or professionally. I always experienced a little cringe in my solar plexus and would avert my eyes when I'd see someone with Down syndrome in the grocery store or walking down the street. Now, I feel like running up and saying, "I know you. I know you." They feel like family. Sadie has opened up a whole world for me, and she has done that for many in our family and circles of friends. She has cracked open a heart that I guess needed cracking, and I am a better person for it. And that is only one of her many gifts to me.

The Gift of Presence

My daughter and granddaughter are two of my most important spiritual teachers. One of the lessons they remind me of, on a daily basis, is the need to be present. Presence is a quality I have valued from the time I first understood what that really meant. In the 80's, I studied Psychosynthesis, a psychospiritual approach to healing and transformation. Toni and Philip Brooks, my now good friends, facilitated the training and, over many months, taught us how to be present and how to help clients be present, as well. Presence was seen as a necessary context for healing to occur. We learned many techniques to help us focus on immediate, direct experience, but the message was always that techniques were secondary. What was most important was how we related to the people we worked with.

To me, being present with another means setting aside my personal agendas, such as the need to fix, to impress, to change, to control, to impose what I think is needed. It means being willing to connect fully with this person in the moment, being faithful to each moment as it unfolds, and working with myself to detach from past experiences or future fantasies, from the busy twistings of the mind, so that I can be right here, right now. I often think of the Zen concept of "Beginner's Mind," which means letting go of agendas and preconceptions, unhooking from distractions and the busy mind, and experiencing each situation, each person, and each moment as fresh and alive. This is a mind that is open to all possibilities and ready for anything, a mind that is curious and without bias. When I am present, I let go of control, as well as attachment to outcomes, and I meet the person I am attending to with my whole self. At these times, the other person feels met.

Another gift of presence is that it gives us greater access to insights and new ideas because we're no longer solely identifying with our rational minds. We open ourselves to deeper knowing and, suddenly, see the solution to a problem or have an insight about our care recipient or their treatment protocol that we hadn't seen before.

The greater my presence, the more I am able to listen fully, attune to and hear what's not being said and what's between the lines, attend to feelings, energies, and subtle cues of which the care recipient may be unaware. I become more attuned because ego is out of the way, and I am able to see others as they really are, not as I wish or expect them to be. We relax and often feel good about ourselves when we are empathically heard and fully met.

We often feel safe. We feel better about ourselves when we're not being judged or controlled. We feel appreciated, in fact, loved. This can go a long way toward facilitating any healing.

Maintaining presence, however, is not easy to do. One evening, when Heidi was in a lot of pain in her lower back and rib cage due to a flare-up of Ankylosing Spondylitis, I offered some "motherly advice." This time it was about some nutritional supplement for pain that someone told me about. She turned to me with a strained look on her face and burst out crying. "Mom," she cried out, "please, just love me. Just be here with me while I'm hurting. Just be here. Please, just be here. Just love me right now." I stopped in that moment. I saw how my advice-giving, brilliant ideas, and suggestions were rarely what she needed. She had plenty of doctors who could take care of that. She needed my full presence, not my fear-driven remedies. That was a turning point for me. She might just as well have been a Zen monk in my living room, exhorting me to Wake Up!

How Helping Others Helps You

Another gift of Heidi's illnesses and Sadie's Down syndrome in my life is my understanding of the power and transformative effects of service. Serving another can be an assault on our egos which would have us always focus on ourselves, on what's good for us, what will help us stay safe and secure, what will give us pleasure, what's in it for us: me, me, me—the "me syndrome." Caring for another shatters that conditioning. It's no longer about me. Caring for others is a spiritual path in itself. It is an antidote to our feelings of separateness and isolation. We go beyond our insular boundaries and enter into a soul field with another. We experience our true kinship, not just with this one person, but also with many others. A door opens in us and paves the way for other experiences of interconnectedness. Instead of personality connecting to personality, we become Being connecting to Being.

I feel good, really good, when I show up for Heidi, Sadie, my friends, clients, and students. Many of the caregivers I've worked with speak of this, as well. Caregiving is heart-opening work, and I think of us as honored to be able to help others in these ways. My serving is not always selfless, and I don't need or expect it to be. Sometimes, my helping is obligatory or, perhaps, I'm more focused on what I'm getting than what I'm giving. My ego can get puffed up. Aren't I special, even holy? Look how self-sacrificing I am! Those inflationary thoughts are okay. I'm a flawed human being with some holes in my psyche that still like to be filled by the illusion of specialness.

I can feel the difference, though, when my ego is involved. I'm not in the open, trusting, flow state that comes with unconditional giving. I'm attached to the results. Are my gifts being appreciated? Am I being recognized for my selflessness? Am I getting back as much as I'm giving? When my soul is in the driver's seat, there is no measuring, no grasping, no busy mind stuff. There is just a simple expression of untainted heart: no strings, no conditions, just love.

Learning to Live in the Mystery

Caregiving confronts us with the need to learn how to live with so many unanswered questions. When will the pain subside? Will the pain subside? Will the treatments be successful? Will this be the right medication? Will she live? For how long? Will he walk again? Will he be able to use his right arm? Will she have a recurrence? Will he be able to tolerate living in a nursing home? How will she handle this latest news? How do I tell her? What will be required of me now?

Stephanie has been in remission for two and a half years since her second recurrence of breast cancer. Her mother, Rose, said that it was only recently that she finally accepted the fact that her daughter's future simply could not be predicted. "When I did that," she said, "I finally relaxed. I've never had an easy time of "not knowing." I hated having to wait for answers to anything. I was decisive and pretty good at analyzing, strategizing, and figuring things out—a good sleuth and problem-solver. I could readily find answers to all kinds of questions. Whether or not they were always accurate didn't matter much. I just found out what I needed to know and was usually fine with that. I guess you could say I was a kind of know-it-all. And I set up my life with as many controllable variables as possible. The unknown was too scary."

Stephanie's mom continued, "This experience with Stephanie has been the most difficult event in my life. I could hardly bear the news of the big C, and all the waiting nearly drove me crazy. First, there was her discovery of the lump in her right breast and the nail-biting waiting for the results of the biopsy. Then came all the decisions about treatments, waiting for more tests, and not knowing what side effects she'd have or how debilitating they'd be. I could never relax with any of it. And the worst waiting of it all is now. Who knows if she'll have another recurrence? If she does, who knows how serious it will be? Who knows if my daughter will live?"

"I had an aha moment about a year ago," Rose said, "that turned this around for me and has actually changed my life. I realized that there are no guarantees about anything. I don't know and cannot know and no one will be able to tell me if Stephanie will live past her fortieth birthday. It's not up to me. There isn't one thing I can do to fix things so the cancer won't come back or to find out how any of this will turn out. I finally accepted the truth—that this was beyond my control. With that realization came a flood of insights about how I'd been arguing with reality my entire life to avoid pain, disaster, and outcomes I simply never thought I could live with. I'd been holding onto everything very tightly, desperately afraid of losing what was important to me, as if controlling myself and everything around me would keep misfortune at bay." We waited in silence for her to gather her thoughts. "Then, somehow, I let go. I told myself, and knew it was true, that Stephanie's future was unknown. I cried a lot then. The things I had used to shield myself from this truth fell away. After that first cry, I felt like a new woman. I felt like a woman instead of a scared little girl who was always running for safety. I started to become more relaxed about everything. Instead of vigilantly walking through each day as if I were walking across a minefield, I saw that pain, loss, and hardship were inevitable, that they were a part of life, a part of every day, and that there was nothing I or anyone else could do to change that. I saw that what I could change were my reactions. I could continue to fight with reality or accept it. I'm no longer consumed by fear and anxiety about Stephanie. I appreciate every moment that she has and that we have together, but I don't hang onto those moments. I let them come and let them go."

We cannot look to the world of form, which is impermanent and ever changing, for our security. We cannot hold back the tides of illness, suffering, and death. What Rose discovered, though, is that we can let go and accept this situation. A great, but often bittersweet, peace comes with that knowing. Our egoic selves resist this reality every day. It's hard to accept the fact that our loved ones will die, that we will lose people, places, and things we cherish, and that we will die. The houses we live in and the ground we stand on are not ours forever. They are on loan. There is great freedom available to us when we come to terms with this, as Rose did.

In 2000, my own "not knowing" lessons took off. I noticed a small lump on my cheek, close to my mouth. A biopsy revealed that it was a malignant tumor. The doctor wouldn't be able to ascertain what type of malignancy the tumor was until I was in surgery, which turned out to be four months later. He also couldn't guarantee that there would be no facial disfigurement because the tumor was so close to my mouth. Also, I wouldn't know until after the surgery if I'd need radiation and/or chemotherapy, or if the surgery would be enough. I was also informed that it was likely that I would have a large irregular facial scar on my face that would be two to three inches long. The plastic surgeon tried to reassure me that it would fade significantly over time. I was so overwhelmed by all of this information that I didn't think to ask what he meant by "time" and "significantly."

After a few days filled with grief, fear, and catastrophic thinking, I knew that I simply had to bring as much wisdom to this experience as I could possibly muster. This was a spiritual challenge. I meditated for over an hour every day for four months and did a lot of soul searching about what I needed to learn as a result of these life tests. Four months to sit with questions as big as these seemed to me like an eternity. I looked at my fears about cancer and potentially debilitating cancer treatments, and did a lot of deep reflection around self-image. What would it be like to have a crooked smile? A large scar on my face? I looked at my attachment to my appearance and fears about pain and discomfort. I used this time to focus completely on my spirituality because I knew that was the only way I could deal with this. Who was I really? What is this attachment to our bodies that creates so much suffering? How do we let go of this attachment when it's tested? I did so much inner work and was determined to let go because I knew I had no choice. By the time I went into surgery, I was prepared for the worst-case scenarios and actually was at peace with all of them. I had truly surrendered to what is and could be. Initially, it seemed impossible to sit with all of this uncertainty, but I learned to accept that I couldn't know until I knew. I learned to make peace with "not knowing."

As it turned out, the malignancy was basal cell carcinoma, not the worst type to have, but not the best either. I didn't need further treatment. My smile was intact, but I did have a large scar, which took a couple of years to fade. When I looked at the scar for the first time in the mirror, I was aghast and burst into tears. It was redder and larger than I imagined it would be. But there was an ironic twist to this experience. The scar was in the shape of a big question mark on its side on my cheek. I'd been gifted with a visible symbol of one of the lessons I needed to learn. "I won't easily forget about 'living in the question,'" I said to myself.

We always want it to be springtime. We desperately cling to pleasure. We do everything possible to maximize comfort and avoid discomfort. We're phobic about pain in this culture. Resistance is usually our first response to pain or difficult news. "This is unwanted. Get rid of it! Fix it! Make it go away!" we cry out. We want blue skies and sunny days. It is a great gift when we come to accept the ever-changing seasons and cycles of life. Birth. Death. Gain. Loss. Pleasure. Pain. It comes and it goes. Can we embrace it all?

Like Rose, I was never comfortable with the unknown. Patience was definitely not one of my virtues. I always needed to know, and I needed to know now! It has been a wonderful gift—albeit gained through painful circumstances—to learn how to move with life rather than impose my will on people and events. I'm more relaxed and can wait for answers and solutions to unfold when the time is right, rather than when I proclaim the time is right. I appreciate questions and the mystery. What a relief! What a gift!

The rewards of caregiving are abundant. At times, they are seemingly small: an expression of gratitude, a patient or friend with a smile on her face, unexpected support, or good news about a prognosis. Personal patterns and behaviors that we have been stuck in for years can fall away, and we start to embody qualities that we've always admired in others but never thought we'd discover in ourselves. We change in both measurable and immeasurable ways, becoming resourceful, strong, compassionate, fearless, resilient, more open, available, and in touch with our feelings. Often, it is hard to see the gifts, and we must not chastise ourselves for that. Caregiving can be the most challenging endeavor we will ever face. Even if hidden, the gifts are there. Acknowledging them is healing for our bodies, minds, and spirits.

EXERCISES AND ACTIVITIES

Writing Exercises—Inquiry and Reflection

Take some time to relax and center yourself before you begin these writing exercises. Then, give yourself five to ten minutes to respond to each one.

1. Consider that your care recipient is a spiritual mentor in your life, teaching you the lessons that you

need for your spiritual growth at this time. What are you learning?

2. What are some of the positive ways that caregiving has changed you? Write about specific examples with regard to the following areas: mind, body, feelings, and spirit.

3. Recall three positive events in the last week related to your experience as a caregiver. For example, your care recipient expressed gratitude about your generosity, or you visited an art gallery as part of your self-care. Take at least a minute to reflect on and savor each one. Let these experiences register in your whole body-mind. In so doing, you are training yourself to receive the good, to let positive experiences deeply imprint your mind, body, and feelings. If you practice this once a week, you will find that you are actually aware of more "bright spots," and they are no longer insignificant events.

Collage Exercise—Soul Gifts Collage Process

For this exercise, you'll need a few magazines, scissors, glue, and a large sheet of drawing paper or poster board.

1. Go through the magazines and look for words and images that represent the gifts of caregiving to you. Let your heart and feelings guide you in this process. Allow yourself to be surprised.

2. Arrange the words and images on the poster board or paper in any way that feels right to you.

3. When you are done, take about twenty minutes and write about your collage. How do you feel as you reflect on the collage? What stands out for you? Do you notice any patterns? Is anything missing that you'd like to add?

4. Add to your collage over the coming days and weeks. Reflect on it from time to time to remind yourself of the gifts of your experiences.

Self-Guided Imagery—Finding the Gifts

1. Find a comfortable place to sit for about fifteen minutes. Adjust your position in any ways that you need to, close your eyes, and let yourself settle into the chair or couch. Bring your awareness to your breathing and follow the breath for two or three minutes, as it comes in and goes out, letting yourself relax as you align with the rhythm of your breathing.

2. Imagine that you're walking into a very nice room, perhaps in your home, or create any kind of room you like in your imagination.

3. A number of wrapped gifts are in the room. Each one has your name on it. What you will find as you open each package is something that represents your particular gifts of caregiving. Unwrap each one, and take your time to reflect on the contents. For example, you may unwrap a red heart and, upon reflection, discover that you have truly become more loving as a result of your experience. A heart may represent different things to different people. Be curious and open to what a heart show-

ing up at this time uniquely means to you. Particular instances may come to mind of experiences in your caregiving that were instrumental in creating this shift in you. Objects or aspects of nature may be in the boxes. You may also find words: for example, strength, patience, or acceptance in your packages.

4. When you feel complete, take a few minutes to jot down what you discovered.

5. Repeat this process whenever you want to. Different gifts may appear, and certainly, as you cultivate new qualities in yourself and experience more rewards from your caregiving, new packages will appear.

Chapter 2

BOULDERS ON THE PATH: THE STRESSORS OF CAREGIVING

Caregiver stress. Burnout. Compassion fatigue. What makes caregiving so stressful? What are the challenges? How can you successfully work with them? How can you prevent burnout? How can you reduce and manage stress? How do you cope?

Years ago, I was a participant in a writing workshop, and our first assignment was to write about something current in our lives that had an "edge" for us. We read our pieces aloud. I wrote about Heidi's recent diagnoses and the toll this was taking on me. At the lunch break, Jonathan, a psychiatrist, took me aside. "Crohn's is a difficult disease to manage," he said. "Its course is highly unpredictable, which you're already experiencing. The combination of A.S. and Crohn's is really a lot to handle. This can consume a family. Be sure to take care of yourself." His eyes were penetrating, and his voice and demeanor serious. His comments and the care he expressed took me by surprise. I was moved by our exchange. As a result of our conversation, I started feeling more worried about myself than I had been. I became anxious about what might be in my future.

I vacillated between hopeful self-talk and doom and gloom scenarios. On the one hand, it was, "She'll get over this. We'll find the right treatment. There are so many alternative treatments available if traditional medicine isn't effective. They could find a cure while she's still young. Thank God this isn't some other more debilitating disease. She's looked and felt better lately. Maybe this is the end of relapses." On the other hand, images would flash before my eyes of Heidi in emergency rooms and hospitals for the rest of her life, having to live with a colostomy bag that she'd hate, getting bloated and sick from being on steroids, wasting away from weight loss, and other ghastly possibilities. The gravity with which Jonathan spoke to me triggered my fear and catastrophic thinking. His warning—that a serious, chronic illness can consume a family, let alone an individual caregiver—is something that all of us who are caregivers need to heed. His pointing to the imperative of self-care is one of the reasons I wrote this book.

Professional and family caregivers share many of the same challenges. These include emotional difficulties, physical demands, time pressure, financial issues, lack of adequate support, emotional and behavioral problems in care receivers, and problems with the interface with your care recipients' friends and family members. You put in long, hard hours. Most of you are overworked. Many of you are stretched beyond your emotional and physical capacities. Confronting pain and suffering on an ongoing basis can be highly stressful. In addition, you receive limited recognition for all that you do. The focus, understandably, is primarily on the patient. Your feelings, needs, and difficulties are often invisible, at times, even to yourselves.

Emotional Challenges

Jeanette, a heart surgeon, said, "There's neither time nor place for feelings in this environment. Also, exhibiting feeling is seen as unprofessional. We do take that part of caring home with us. I think most health care practitioners are in denial about the impact on their own health of not having a place to confront their feelings. They barrel through and do their best to dissociate from what they're feeling. I was fortunate enough to have a colleague tell me that I was on the verge of burnout and needed help. I knew it. I was apathetic, having trouble sleeping, was becoming increasingly short-tempered and impatient— even with patients, and had fallen back into overeating. Luckily, I was willing to take what he told me seriously before it was too late."

The emotional challenges of caregiving can be daunting. As a caregiver, at times I still wish that I were one of those people who had more of a Teflon-like personality so things could easily roll off me. Heidi used to tell me that I needed to have "thicker skin." I do have good boundaries now, and I am much more resilient than I was in the early period of her illnesses, but still, I'm a softy in many ways. I'm a sensitive, feeling type. If I hear a baby crying in a restaurant, I have an urge to rush over there to soothe her. I can hardly bear to see an animal being mistreated. When Heidi looks particularly tired or is in a lot of pain, I can still get a knot in my solar plexus and shift into worry mode. For the most part, I have come to accept my sensitive nature and, most importantly, to respect and take care of it. If I'm triggered, I no longer judge myself for having thin skin. I check in with myself to see what I need and what I may need to do to become balanced again. Sometimes, it's as simple as taking a short walk. At other times, I take out the journal I always keep with me for times like these. I write out my feelings. I may call my husband or one of my wonderful, caring friends for support.

I don't schedule too many sessions in a day. I take short breaks frequently to breathe deeply, stretch, or do some self-guided imagery. Even a few minutes can refresh me. If I'm going to visit Heidi and the kids and one of them is sick or I know something is going on that might stretch me emotionally, I bookend, that is, I set up a nurturing activity on both sides of the visit. Perhaps, I'll meditate before I go to their house so I'll be calm and centered when I'm there and, then, treat myself to a healthy pleasure, like a nice dinner, when I leave.

If you are a hearty, resilient type already, these measures may not be necessary for you. Perhaps, a great emotional challenge for you is to be faced with so many situations you cannot control. You may have little impact with regard to how your care recipient responds to any treatment, how they progress, if they progress, how they feel, what they think, or how they react to you or anyone else. We cannot control how quickly the many bureaucratic systems we have to contend with will move along. Unexpected losses of support, diminishing resources, and our own physical and emotional health are just some of the things that may present themselves and not have easy solutions. As caregivers, we often have to participate in difficult decisions where there are many differences of opinion. You may feel powerless quite often and very frustrated because of that.

Lynn, a hospice nurse, said that she was constantly faced with hard choices. "Many of my patients thrive on having visitors, but they tire so easily, especially when the people who visit them don't know how to be with someone who's dying. They talk on and on; some of them ask a million questions. I have to decide whether or not it's better for the patients to have fewer visitors or to have visitors spend less time in the room or just let them be surrounded by people who care about them. I have to decide which is better for the patient, and I'm not always sure I'm making the right decision. Pain medication is yet another story. It can make them dizzy, anxious, or confused, but it relieves the physical pain. In their final days, what's most important?"

It is no small task to continuously be in the presence of suffering. As caregivers, we watch our clients and those we love in nearly unbearable physical or emotional pain, or both, at times. We sit with people as they lose their faculties—their ability to walk, move, see, and hear. They may be frightened or anxious. Our care recipients have setbacks; they fail to respond to treatments. We witness the grief and fear of the family members and friends of our care receivers. Emotional overload is not uncommon for health care professionals, as well as family caregivers. "The hardest thing for me about being a psychotherapist," said Harry, "is not only constantly witnessing the current emotional distress that my clients are in, but also hearing one story after another of unfathomable losses and abuses. I'm frequently in awe of how they survived at all." Our own painful memories can be triggered by our care receivers' experiences. Any significant loss or traumatic event in our lives can be reawakened when we are exposed to deep suffering in another person. I was visiting a colleague who was in hospice, and she was experiencing intense fears about dying. Her psychic pain awakened painful memories in me about my father in the weeks before he died. I was able to bracket the material that was being activated in me and deal with it later by writing in my journal. It's very important for you to have tools to work with the emotions that may get stirred up in you when you are helping others.

Time Pressure

I have yet to meet a professional or family caregiver who feels like they have enough time for all that is on their plates. Competing demands for time, long hours, and conflicting priorities all exert pressure. Time constraints often plague psychotherapists, social workers, physicians, and nurse practitioners, who work in designated time slots and have full caseloads. Whatever is going on with the client or patient can be handled only in that fifteen or, perhaps, fifty-minute session.

Many of you who are friend and family caregivers juggle work, family, and caregiver responsibilities, often feeling that you don't have enough quality time to devote to any one area. Genevieve, a single mother, is an elementary school teacher and mother of a nine-year-old son who has cystic fibrosis. "Nothing's getting done to my satisfaction," she said. "The most important thing to me is to be fully available to Charlie, but I have to work. I teach kindergarten, and these children can sense when I'm not fully present. They act out or pull on me for attention. I'm unable to be present if I've had a hard day with Charlie, which is happening a lot lately. Then, I come home from a trying day with them, and it's hard to be there for Charlie in the ways he needs. I'm overwhelmed, and the smallest things are getting to me."

Many of you feel as if you have lost your personal lives altogether. Maneuvering through the health care maze and sometimes having to deal with legal entanglements is burdensome and time consuming. Caregiving professionals are bogged down with paperwork. Many health care practitioners bemoan the fact that they don't have time to tend to their patients' family members, including time to consult with them as to how they might assist with the patient's care. Unexpected crises frequently disrupt plans and schedules. Corrina, a home health aide, said that she lies awake at night thinking about priorities and schedules. "I get up, ready to put the latest plan into action; then, inevitably, something happens to foul things up. I have to be flexible every moment of every day. And many things just don't get done. I do get to most, if not all, of the really important things. But I used to think everything on my many lists was important. I've sure had to let go of that one!"

Issues of Care Recipients

As so many of you know, the experience of any serious emotional or physical illness is highly stressful for the person who is ill or disabled. Their stress can greatly impact you. In addition to the debilitating symptoms of the condition, patients are often afraid, angry, confused, depressed, or anxious. Our care receivers often feel helpless. Their lives may feel out of control. You may also feel helpless and out of control if you are unable to provide relief. They are no longer in charge of their own lives, perhaps reliant on others for the first time since they were young children. They may be pressured financially. Due to their health, they may be unable to work or need to work less. Medical expenses are likely to increase, and the possibility of decreasing income looms large. A mother may be ill and unable to care for her children as she did before. A teenager, who is trying to become independent, suddenly finds himself as dependent on his family as he was when he was a toddler. Many worry about being a burden to those around them. People with a diagnosis of cancer or heart disease may feel bad about themselves, believing they caused their illness by unhealthy eating habits, not following doctors' orders, being forgetful about taking medications, smoking, or refusing to accept particular treatments. They chastise themselves for working too hard, neglecting self-care, living a less than healthy lifestyle. People with injuries will often criticize themselves for driving recklessly, not wearing a helmet on their bike, or taking too many risks. A typical statement is: "I should have …, could have …, why didn't I …, I can't forgive myself for …, if only I had listened to …" Self-blame is common.

The experience of helplessness is common in people with life-altering illnesses. This is especially true for people who are used to managing their own lives, being independent and self-sufficient, and feeling in control much of the time. Now, they are face-to-face with something that has many aspects that are beyond their control. They discover that they can't just will themselves through this life event. Suddenly, or more gradually, they find themselves with less energy, unable to move at the speed they are used to, having to slow down, or contend with pain or uncomfortable side effects from medications or treatments. They have diminished use of their faculties, are confined to being indoors, in bed, or perhaps in a wheel chair. Simple tasks take longer or cannot be managed at all. This person may have been afraid for years of ever being weak or helpless. Rarely having needed to rely on others for very much, now they must depend on others even for the bare essentials. This is difficult to accept. If this appears to be more than a temporary state of affairs, your care recipient may be deeply upset. Their distress may be difficult for you to manage.

Glenn, age thirty-eight, turned left at a busy intersection on a red light. He was blindsided on the driver's side of his car by a large truck, knocked unconscious, and trapped in the car. While in the hospital with a severe subdural hematoma—a hemorrhage in the brain, for two weeks, even though conscious, he didn't know who he was. When he regained his memory and left the hospital, Glenn was not the clear-headed and "take charge" man that he had been before the accident. This was devastating for him. He was frustrated, angry, and, at times, depressed. Glenn had become very emotional, and he was someone who had always kept his emotions in check. "I refused to accept my inability to consistently think clearly and to be a hostage of my emotions. And I wouldn't ask anyone for help," he said. "I was in a relationship and kept resisting my partner's attempts to help me. Friends and family reached out, as well, and I wanted none of it. I pushed everyone away. My relationship ended about a year later, and my business failed, as well." Looking back, Glenn regrets not allowing his family or partner to support him in ways he knows now, over twenty years later, would have been helpful.

People with life-altering conditions frequently have to deal with fear. Initially, there is the shock and disbelief when a diagnosis is pronounced. "I was completely taken aback," said Maureen, upon learning in her mid-fifties that she had thyroid cancer. "Nothing prepared me for this. I had been feeling fine, just a bit more tired than usual. I thought I'd just been working too hard and getting a little older like everyone else I know. After I got over the shock, terror set in. "Oh my God," I thought. "This is serious—really serious. I was afraid of everything—pain and disability, costly medical treatments, losing income from not being able to work, maybe losing my job altogether, having to rely on my family and friends, and on and on. I couldn't see anything but my fear."

After the initial fears, the whole experience of dealing with life-altering illness is fraught with many things that can potentially activate other fears. Will I ever regain my health? Will my condition worsen? Will this or that treatment be effective? Can I handle the side effects? How will I pay the medical bills? Other bills? Many patients worry about recurrences and every new ache and pain. Many are afraid of the impact their illness will have on the people they care about. "How can Diane handle this?" asked her partner, Shelley. "She has the kids to take care of, and her Mom's not doing great. Now me. I can't bear the thought of adding to her burden."

We all deal with fear differently. People who are aware that they are afraid and have tools and support for processing their feelings are more likely to handle their emotions with more ease than those who don't. This doesn't mean that these people have an easier time emotionally. It just means that their feelings are on the surface and can be dealt with more directly. Many people with serious illnesses are in denial about how frightened they really are. Fear isn't easy to admit or accept. At times, your care recipients will lash out at you, their doctors, family, or friends. They may withdraw and be difficult to reach. They may resort to all kinds of coping strategies: minimizing the impact of the illness in their life, blaming others for their fate, becoming bitter, resentful, and perhaps despondent. These reactions can be very difficult for you as caregivers to handle. At times like these, it is wise to consult with the patient's doctor or other qualified professionals.

The Stress of Dealing with Your Care Recipient's Family and Friends

In addition to being stressed by emotional and behavioral challenges in care recipients, the interface with family members and friends of care receivers poses a set of potential obstacles for you. When one person is sick or disabled, the whole family and/or circle of friends is affected. Serious illness is a family event, and part of caregiving is interacting, and often working closely with, the people who are close to your care receiver. Just as the patient is stressed, so are those close to him or her. People are very worried, sometimes overwhelmed, about this very difficult situation. So much may change, and many of us don't take easily to change.

Roles and responsibilities often change. If a parent is ill, suddenly the adult children take on parenting roles. Your older sister, who was more like the mother of the family than your actual mother was, is sliding into dementia, and now, one or more siblings become caregivers. A good friend who has been your fun and movie buddy is diagnosed with bipolar disorder and, increasingly now, needs as much help as you can provide because she lives far away from family.

Everyone's emotions may be constantly shifting and unpredictable. People are touchy and irritable, sometimes feeling guilty, often not knowing how to manage their turbulent emotional states. They are frightened as they behold the suffering of someone they care about. Tempers flare. People's usual responses to stress often become exaggerated. Some withdraw, retreat into a shell. Others become compulsive "doers," frenetically busy with details and activities, some of which are important, others which are not. Some turn to alcohol or other substances to help them cope. Under all of the coping mechanisms, family and friends usually feel just as helpless as the patient does. At times, the care receiver's family and friends will displace their frustration and take it out on caregivers. "It's your fault that she's not getting better," screamed Vicky to her friend's nurse. "It's your job to save her life, and she's getting worse every day."

Lee, a surgical nurse, said that it is common for friends and relatives to blame nurses and physicians for whatever's going wrong. "We're supposed to be the saviors. You just can't take this personally if you want to survive in this profession."

Family Ties and Knots

Healthy children in families where a sibling is seriously ill can suffer a lot. Not only is it just as difficult for them to see their brother or sister in physical or emotional pain, but they also tend to receive less attention than the child with the observable symptoms. It's not unusual for these children to start having problems at school or develop stress-related symptoms themselves. Also, the predictable family routines and patterns of relating change. The home environment no longer feels as stable and secure as it once did. In addition, the other children's struggles add additional stress to the already stressed parents. These issues, if not addressed, can lead to further problems.

Underlying jealousy, power struggles, competition, resentments, and other unresolved family dynamics often surface when there is a health crisis in a family. Sometimes there is competition with regard to who is doing the most or who is doing the best job. There may be jealousy because a parent is again favoring the daughter who was favored as a child. Another common situation that arises is that the person who is providing the most care may expect that other family members contribute their fair share. When they don't pitch in, resentment is common. Families have to answer important and difficult questions. Who will be the primary caregiver? Why this person and not someone else? What will these responsibilities consist of? How will other family members participate? If there are financial concerns, who will take responsibility for them? If a family or support system is relatively healthy and there is good communication, many of these issues can be worked through without a lot of conflict and distress. To the degree, though, that a family has unresolved emotional issues, these concerns can become trouble spots of turmoil, disagreement, resentment, and unhappiness for all concerned.

"I didn't speak to my brother for almost two years after Pops died," said Ernesto. "I just couldn't forgive him for turning his back on Mom and me and letting us do everything. He sent a check every month to help cover the extra expenses, and he'd call Pops a couple of times a month. But he didn't lift a finger to help out. He'd never been one to contribute much to the family, except with money and gifts, so I guess I shouldn't have expected much no matter how sick our father was. But I did. This seemed different. It was the first time we really needed him. We told him that, and he said he'd get more involved, like he'd said before about other things. But he didn't. When I did decide to talk to him again, we had it out. He opened up for the first time and said he never felt like Pops loved him like he loved me, so he pulled away years ago. I understood him for the first time."

Different friends and family members may have conflicting ideas and expectations about how you should be serving the care recipient. After surgery, Aunt Eva wants you to put all your attention on pain management and her brother Robert's comfort, while Robert's daughter is more concerned with getting him to move and begin to walk.

Serious illness can also bring out the best in family relationships and in communities. At times, whole communities band together to help an ailing member. Heidi is in a twelve-step recovery community, and the members of her program have consistently showed up to help Heidi out when she experiences health difficulties, as she does for them. As soon as they found out that she was going to have a baby with Down syndrome, they gathered around her to welcome Sadie with loving arms, and still do, to help out whenever assistance is needed. Over thirty of these "recovery friends" attended a baby shower before Sadie was born, and Heidi said that they expressed the most heartfelt sentiments she'd ever heard. They were in a circle and, one by one, each person came up to her, some putting their arms around her, some holding her hands in theirs, and each spoke deeply and authentically from their souls. Not an eye was dry in that room. You are fortunate, indeed, if your care recipient has a community of supporters around him or her.

Some families are able to put their personal differences aside to serve whoever is ill in the highest possible ways. The whole family may come together in ways that it never has. After eleven years of marriage, Jules and Margot divorced. While living separately and co-parenting, their eight-year-old daughter, Julia, was diagnosed with juvenile diabetes. The family met this challenge in ways that no one could have predicted. Jules and Margot resolved to put their daughter first and to be the best people they could be to serve Julia. "She comes first in a very big way now," said Jules. "Everything else is starting to look pretty petty." Also, there had been numerous unresolved conflicts from the past and underlying tension between the mothers-in-law. They, too, at Jules and Margot's prompting, were able to see the importance of uniting as a family and to treat Julia's health as a family problem that required everyone to walk in "bigger shoes." In this case, serious illness precipitated major healing in the family, which, in turn, lessened stressors for the caregivers.

This chapter has presented many of the potential stressors of caregiving. What follows are guidelines and techniques for managing stress and working with challenges. Throughout the book, you will find numerous ideas and suggestions to support you in self-care, the number one solution to the problem of "caregiver burnout."

EXERCISES AND ACTIVITIES

Guidelines for Managing Stress

1. You need to recognize that you are stressed if you are. That may sound obvious, but many caregivers are in denial about the physical and emotional toll that caregiving may be taking on them. Symptoms of stress may include fatigue, anxiety, agitation, worry, feeling overwhelmed, irritability, inability to concentrate, sleep disturbances, digestive problems, increase in, or loss of appetite.

2. Realize that what is stressful for one person is not for another, and what relieves stress for one person may not be helpful for someone else. Witnessing uncontrolled pain may be difficult for you, but not as challenging as seeing your care recipient in deep despair. The opposite may be true for someone else.

    Identify what is uniquely stressful for you. Don't compare yourself to others. Stressors can be internal or external. An example of an internal stressor is self-criticism. It is taxing on your body-mind to repeatedly berate yourself for not being good or kind enough or to be unforgiving of yourself if you make mistakes. Examples of external stressors might be difficult interactions with medical personnel or family members, your care recipient directing anger toward you, or being overloaded with too many tasks.

3. Identify the ways that you typically respond to stress. What are your patterns? This may be

uncomfortable to consider, but it's important that you are clear so that you can see exactly what change needs to happen and what new behaviors can be put in place. Be as specific as possible and willing to look honestly at your common reactions. For example, do you withdraw and isolate yourself, perhaps putting up walls between you and others? Do you turn to addictive substances or behaviors like food, alcohol, drugs, or hours at the computer to escape your discomfort? Do you take your feelings out on others, including your care recipient? Do you try to lose yourself in excessive busyness?

4. Have a clear intention and make a commitment to manage your stress in healthy new ways. Tell yourself, perhaps in writing, why it is imperative for you to make this a priority if, in fact, it is. If you find that you are telling yourself that you don't have enough time, stop those thoughts quickly. Tell yourself you will find the time because this is so important.

5. When you have some time, sit down and explore your feelings. Beneath many of your reactive responses are feelings that you may have been unconsciously trying to avoid. We often think that giving attention to painful feelings means we'll become engulfed by them. It's actually the resistance to feelings that keeps us stuck and has us acting out in self-sabotaging ways. You may be reaching for chocolate cake, for example, to avoid grief, or zoning out in front of the TV so that you don't have to face your fear. Feeling leads to healing. I like the saying, "What you feel, you can heal."

Good questions to ask yourself are: What am I afraid to feel? What am I afraid will happen if I let myself feel? How do I distract myself from feeling?

As caregivers, you need healthy ways to express the whole range of feelings you're likely to experience. Writing and journaling techniques can be used to process feelings. (See Chapter Six—The Write Way to Well-Being.) Free drawing is another powerful tool for emotional expression and release. With a blank piece of paper and colored pens beside you, let your hand draw whatever feeling is present for you. While you're drawing, try not to think about what you're drawing or whether or not it is a "good" drawing. As your hand moves on the paper, it's likely that feelings will surface. Insights may also arise for you.

You can also move or dance your feelings. Stand in your living room, and give yourself permission to let grief or frustration move through you in any way that happens naturally. You may find yourself shaking, reaching, or pushing away. Perhaps you gently place your hand over your heart. Let movements occur rather than trying to control the ways your body wants to express itself.

Other techniques to allow for emotional discharge include letting yourself scream in the car on the freeway, when you're alone at the beach, or into a pillow. A friend of mine has a punching bag that he uses to vent his anger. Running, aerobic exercise, and throwing or kicking balls can also be cathartic.

If your feelings become too intense, though, or you simply don't feel safe accessing this material on your own, it is wise to seek professional help.

6. Identify people, places, and activities that deplete you. This may be difficult to do, especially if some of these people are old friends, colleagues, or family members. It is easy to be in denial about the deleterious effects that people have on us, especially if they are people who have been in our lives for a long time and who would be upset if we turned our backs on them. As a caregiver, though, you can't afford to deny the impact on your mental, emotional, physical, and spiritual well-being of everything you're doing in your life—how you spend your time and everyone that you connect with. Avoiding toxic people, places, and things is necessary as it is likely that you need more strength, resilience, and energy than ever before.

When you have a choice, be particularly careful not to spend time with people who undermine you. They may be jealous or resentful of the time you are giving to caregiving or judgmental of how you are doing your job. They may try to manipulate or control you, or endlessly criticize you for doing too much or not enough. They think they know what is right and you don't. These issues are common. They can certainly be communicated and worked out much of the time, especially if both parties are willing to talk and to look at their own participation in the difficulty. It is more important than ever, though, not to sweep the truth of the influence of this negativity and lack of support under the rug. Caregiving can catalyze unfinished business in families and friendships, bringing issues to the surface that may have been buried for years. This is both a curse and a blessing—a curse because the eruption of feelings and issues that have been underground is confrontive and painful, and a gift because herein lies an opportunity for healing and transformation.

Make a list of people, places, and activities that are draining for you. Write about or reflect on each item on the list, being as honest with yourself as you can. This acknowledgement is an important first step in getting clear. As you reflect on your list, you may discover that change is required. Some difficult conversations may lie ahead. Some people's feelings may be hurt. You may be rejected or further criticized. It may become clear that visiting the mall a couple of times a week has been stimulating, but not at all satisfying, or that watching the evening news every night is actually adding stress to your life.

7. Create a Soul Nourishment Toolkit. If you feed your soul what it deeply needs, you will feel replenished and fulfilled, with a greater ability to fulfill your caregiving roles and responsibilities and to weather the unpredictable storms of caregiving. Make a list of soul friends, sacred places, and life-affirming activities. Who listens to you wholeheartedly and cares about what you say and feel? Who makes your heart sing? Who believes in you? Write the names of people you trust and those who have your best interests at heart.

Consider where you feel alive and centered. Think about the places both in and outside of your home, or the home of your care recipient, that nourish your soul. If a certain corner of your bedroom or the open space nearby is a sanctuary for you, go there often.

What activities contribute to your well-being? In addition to the activities you're already aware of—like gardening, running, or playing the guitar, list other activities that you sense could be fun or nurturing, for example, going to the museum, the beach, or spending an hour at a bookstore.

Keep this list close by, and add to it whenever you feel drawn to do that. The more possibilities you have on any given day, the better. Do what you love, as often as you can. Spending five or ten minutes in your busy caregiving day talking to a soul friend or reading a chapter in a novel by your favorite author can give you the boost you need.

8. Celebrate the positive moments. Take them in. There are usually many bright spots, even in a very difficult situation or day. As caregivers, we tend to overlook them because they pale in comparison to the difficulties we are contending with. Acknowledging an expression of gratitude that your care recipient extended to you or the fact that an interaction with a family member went more smoothly than you expected is worthy of celebration. The fact that you went for a walk or wrote in your journal instead of sitting at the computer is a wonderful accomplishment.

Registering the experience in your imagination and your whole body-mind helps to deepen the imprint of positive experiences. You're letting them come all the way in. This increases your capacity to receive good feelings and happiness. You will find that your ability to appreciate beauty, goodness, and joy will be enhanced, and you will start noticing how many shiny moments you actually do experience on a given day. The many simple treasures and pleasures that we hardly notice or take for granted seem to start showing up everywhere. We feel happier and life starts to look brighter. Establish realistic time frames and goals. If your goals aren't attainable, you are setting yourself up for failure, disappointment, and more stress. Setting realistic goals helps you stay focused and in control. Having good time management skills goes a long way in helping caregivers experience more ease and less pressure.

9. Know your triggers. For example, if a particular family member consistently "gets under your skin" when he or she comes to visit, prepare in advance for this event as much as possible. Perhaps you can plan to be out of the room for a while, or you can take a walk or meditate before you see this person. If you notice yourself becoming tense or frustrated in their presence, don't let those feelings build up. Take a few deep breaths, or remove yourself from the situation for a few minutes to regain your composure. If you weren't able to modify your reaction to the stressor, don't wait too long to do something to bring yourself back into balance.

Make a list of what commonly triggers you in your caregiving situation. Make another list of strategies you can employ on the spot if you do get activated.

10. Accept the fact that there are situations and events you cannot control. This isn't easy to do, especially in a culture that gives us messages that we can and should master any situation. We can control how we respond to stress, but there is a lot that we, as caregivers, deal with that is beyond our control. Becoming clear about what can be changed and what can't is helpful here.

11. Know what is your responsibility and what isn't with regard to your caregiving duties. As caregivers, many of us take on more than we should or need to, and this simply adds to the experience of emotional and physical overload.

12. Awaken your senses.

- Sight. Place images that uplift, calm, or inspire you in places where you will regularly see them. Use colors to enliven your surroundings. Discover what you love to look at, what brings you pleasure, what is beautiful to you. Perhaps, it is plants or flowers, sacred objects, beautiful stones, mirrors, paintings, or sculpture. Feast your eyes on beauty.

- Sound. Music evokes different feeling states. Use music to experience joy, and to energize or relax you. If you love the sound of water, put a small fountain in your bedroom. You can get recordings of the sounds of nature, which is perfect if you're not able to get to the ocean or the mountains.

- Scent. Fragrances can enhance your moods. Don't just smell the scents; inhale each fragrance deeply. Citrus and peppermint can energize and refresh you. Lavender, sandalwood, and vanilla can soothe your nerves. Notice the effect of different scents on your emotional states. Add fragrant flowers, a bowl of fresh fruit, scented candles, incense, potpourri, or oils to your environment.

- Touch. Massages are deeply relaxing and wonderful for relieving stress. In addition to receiving a massage, you can give yourself a neck, hand, or head massage. Perhaps a cool shower will revive you, or a warm bath will help calm you. For many people, petting a dog or cat is soothing. Animals can also evoke feelings of love and tenderness.

- Taste. What tastes are most pleasing to you? When you eat these foods, savor each bite. Take your time. Eat and drink slowly. Pay attention to your enjoyment of the food.

- Pause many times a day. As often as you can, shift your attention to anything that is relaxing and pleasurable. Awaken your senses when you pause. Take the experience in; savor it. Let your whole body-mind receive the positive feelings that accompany this experience. Even one or two minutes of looking out the window at trees or the expansive blue sky, listening to birds or soothing music can calm or uplift you. This also continuously reminds you of the resources you have within you and all around you.

Self-Guided Imagery—Practices for Relieving Stress

Before each of these practices, whenever possible find a quiet and comfortable place to sit. Take a few slow, deep breaths, and close your eyes.

1. Choose a quality that you want to experience. For example, you are tired and want to feel refreshed. Select an aspect of nature that represents this quality, such as a waterfall. Close your eyes and imagine that you are there by the waterfall. Imagine this as vividly as possible. See and feel yourself waking up, coming alive, feeling invigorated.

2. Imagine being in a pleasant natural environment and seeing, hearing, touching, smelling and, perhaps, tasting what is around you. If you are in a meadow, feel the warmth of the sun against your skin, hear birds, touch the bark on a tree trunk, pick an apple from a tree and taste it.

3. To evoke the experience of being comforted, bring to mind someone who loves you. Imagine that he or she is looking into your eyes, feel them holding or hugging you, perhaps soothing you, and hear the sound of their voice expressing their care for you. Take this in deeply.

4. Recall a time that you were deeply relaxed. Relive that experience as if it were happening now. Take deep breaths as you do this. Experience the physical sensations of relaxation from your head to your toes.

5. Think of a color that represents whatever quality you want to evoke, for example, peacefulness,

aliveness, or equanimity. Imagine that you are resting in a bubble of this color and that you are floating in the sky. With each breath, you take in this color, and this quality is awakened in you.

6. Imagine that you are in a place that feels very good to you—a room in your home or a lovely place in nature. Find a place to sit, and invite a symbol that represents your inner wisdom to come and be with you. This symbol could appear as a wise sage, an animal, or even a ray of sunlight. Ask your wisdom figure for advice. What do I need to become balanced? What will relieve this stress? What is causing this stress? Ask any other questions that are relevant to you.

7. Imagine that you are at a fork in the road. One path goes off to the left, another to the right. First, you walk along the left path, and you find a huge box or waste container. Put whatever you want to release into this box or container: fatigue, frustration, irritability. You may imagine that you're putting words, feelings, or images that represent what you want to let go of into the receptacle. Experience this as vividly as possible. When you feel complete, walk back down the path, and return to the fork. Now, walk along the right path. What you find on the right path is a large box that contains images, feelings, or words that represent what you want to experience, for example, calm, resilience, groundedness, pleasure. You may discover a rainbow, a cup of soup, sunshine, or something you love in the container. There may be many items or just one or two. Take them out and spend time fully engaging with each one. Let yourself be filled up by this experience.

Chapter 3

WHERE YOU END AND I BEGIN: BOUNDARIES

In 1985, about five months into my first counseling internship, I found myself becoming irritable and tired, sometimes exhausted, at the end of the day after seeing clients. There were no other notable stressors in my life at the time, and I couldn't figure out what was so draining about this work that I had always thought I'd love to do. I would come to the counseling center in the morning feeling pretty energetic and centered, and often leave feeling cranky and out-of-sorts. I brought this concern to my clinical supervisor, who then watched me work with clients through a two-way mirror. "You're a classic merger," she said. "You're empathetic, which is wonderful, but you don't have clear, firm boundaries. You lean into your clients; you lose yourself. You're merging with them and taking on their feelings and absorbing their energy. You need to have a clear sense of where you end and they begin. It's important to learn how to be open and attuned to your clients and, at the same time, maintain a healthy distance. Learning how to stay connected to yourself while being open, attuned, and connected to your clients will serve you and your clients very well. You also need to stay grounded in your body. We'll do some mock sessions, and I'll teach you grounding techniques and show you ways to remain connected to yourself while relating to your clients. You'll find that you can maintain your own energy and sense of yourself and also be more neutral and objective with clients. I'm going to teach you ruthless compassion."

In addition to learning somatic processes and other practical strategies for developing boundaries, I began exploring and working with deeper unresolved issues that I felt were related to the "boundary problem," such as my need to please, fears of abandonment, difficulty in saying "no" to people, and setting limits. This personal growth work was transformational, and what I learned over the following year impacted all of my relationships in new and healthy ways.

In the initial months of practicing containment and learning how to have clear boundaries, I felt aloof, somewhat reserved. I was hypervigilant, careful not to lose myself in others lest I fell back into the pattern I was trying to change. I had seen this tendency in others who were learning containment. The pendulum may swing in the opposite direction until we feel confident in our ability to naturally express this new way of being without trying so hard to do so. Often, when it comes to boundaries, we eventually find a comfortable place in the middle – not too firm, not too permeable. In addition, I noticed that I became concerned that clients would feel that I didn't care about them if I stepped back, as I was learning to do. I was worried that they'd feel abandoned, neglected. I looked at this deeply and carefully and came to discover that I was projecting. What I was assuming they would feel was what I commonly experienced when someone backed away from me and I didn't want them to. I easily interpreted abandonment if someone established boundaries with me that I didn't want them to set.

This self-inquiry led to deep personal work that ultimately helped me set boundaries with clients without triggering a lot of concern about their responses. I also discovered how powerful projection is and how important it is to check out my assumptions about what people are thinking and feeling whenever possible.

Caregivers and the Importance of Maintaining Boundaries

Boundaries enable us to have a sense of ourselves; they delineate where we end and someone else begins. They allow us to identify our differences from others and to acknowledge that we have separate perceptions, thoughts, and feelings. Boundaries help us identify which emotions belong to us and which don't. In addition, it is easier to deflect emotions that aren't ours if our boundaries are intact. We know who we are in relation to others when we have healthy boundaries. We can respond to others from a place of clarity and strength. Ideally, boundaries are permeable and flexible; they change in response to different situations and to the way we feel at particular times. Boundaries give us a foundation for healthy relating.

Unhealthy boundaries are either too loose or too rigid, and some people vacillate between the two, with fixed boundaries in some situations and overly permeable boundaries in others. In an attempt to protect herself from her father's incessant demands and constant barrage of critical comments, Ramona—a caregiver for her eighty-seven-year-old father, who had pancreatic cancer—built a wall around herself that was most apparent whenever she was in her father's presence.

"I don't know any other way to fend off his attacks. Nothing I do is good enough. I feel distant and uptight when I'm around him and can barely be in the room at times. I know the family thinks I'm cold and uncaring. This wall isn't only keeping me distant from Dad and the rest of the family, but it also keeps me from knowing what's really going on with me. I'm aware lately that I feel so helpless in the face of all this. I don't know where to turn. Behind this wall, I'm angry and I'm scared."

Ramona's suffering and the great difficulty of this situation for all concerned led her to look more deeply at herself. In doing so, she had the insight that, without the wall to protect her, she was afraid she'd be overwhelmed by feelings that she neither wanted to acknowledge to herself nor wanted her family to see. She also realized that if she let herself experience these feelings, which were right below the surface of her awareness, she might suffer less. She was paying a very heavy price for hiding behind this fortress. Her introspection provided her with insights not only into herself, but also into her father's behavior.

"I wonder if some of Dad's anger and frustration is in response to the coldness he gets from me. When I'm around him, I'm like the ice queen. That must feel pretty awful if you're sick."

With these new insights, Ramona's icy demeanor began to thaw, and she was able to get in touch with feelings that had been locked away. She began to soften in her father's presence. Soon, some of his demands became requests, and the critical comments were fewer and less stinging. Gradually, father and daughter both let down their walls and were able to truly meet and see each other for the first time.

Caroline, like me, had boundaries that were too loose. She was highly sensitive, the product of an enmeshed family system where her privacy wasn't respected. "We could never close our bedroom doors all the way, and no one ever knocked before coming in. We weren't allowed to have private phone conversations until we were in high school. When we went out with friends, we had to call every two hours and tell our parents where we were and what we were doing. I never felt like it was okay to have a life of my own," said Caroline.

Caroline was a nurse in a neonatal intensive care unit, and she let herself bond very closely with the newborn infants there, many of whom could have only limited contact with their mothers. "I fall in love with all of them," she said. "These babies are like my own. I think of them at night when I'm not there and even have dreams about them." One of the infants that she had been particularly close to had recently died, and Caroline was devastated by the loss. "I know I shouldn't have gotten this involved, but I couldn't help myself. My husband said that I needed to stop being an emotional sponge. He's right, you know, but I don't have a clue how to do that."

Caroline's awareness about her need for stronger boundaries was a real plus in her favor. It was an important first step towards her healing. Caregivers who are the sensitive, feeling types often feel the need for "thicker skin" and more resilience in the face of emotional and physical pain and loss. Openness and sensitivity are wonderful qualities, but they can also have drawbacks. Caroline had considered doing a different kind of nursing but decided not to make that change until she had done more self-exploration. She did some reading about codependence and boundaries and, as she said, "I saw myself on every page." What she read motivated her to join a codependence recovery group, which helped her to understand some of the root causes of her patterns and to discover creative strategies for healing. She decided to keep her position and, as she told me recently, "I've learned how to detach, with love."

In the bulleted lists below, you will find some common characteristics of the different types of boundaries. Your caregiving can be enhanced if you clearly understand your own tendencies with regard to boundaries. Which characteristics apply to you? Some of you will find that one category applies more to you than the others, and some of you will identify with some characteristics in more than one of the lists, knowing that in certain situations your boundaries are too loose and in others too rigid, and at times healthy. The goal here is to know what constitutes healthy boundaries and to move towards that. At the end of this chapter, you'll find writing exercises for inquiry and reflection and an "Ideal Boundaries Exercise."

Signs of boundaries that are too permeable

- You have difficulty saying "no" to others.

- Your moods change in reaction to the needs of those around you.

- You are easily influenced by others.

- You lose your sense of self when you're around others.

- You don't notice when someone intrudes on your boundaries.

- You're easily distracted by what others are saying or doing.

- You're easily overwhelmed by people.

- You're often unaware of your own wants and needs.

- You have a strong need to please others.

- If someone close to you is experiencing difficulty, you feel it is your responsibility to help them out.

- Your sense of well-being is based on how things are going with others in your relational sphere.

- You compromise your values in order to gain approval or avoid criticism.

Signs of boundaries that are too rigid

- You appear distant or aloof.

- You keep people at a distance.

- You are afraid of being close to others.

- You have difficulty knowing what your needs and feelings are.

- You are uncomfortable sharing feelings and information about yourself with others.

- You don't like to display weakness or helplessness.

- You may be controlling.

- You have fixed ideas and opinions.

- You get feedback that you are "hard to reach."

- You are self-contained.

- At times, you are inflexible and have a hard time compromising with others.

Signs of healthy boundaries

- When appropriate, you let others in.

- You are flexible and adaptable to change.

- You know how to be firm when that's appropriate, but you are not harsh.

- You clearly define and communicate your boundaries with others without feeling guilty or selfish about expressing them.

- You know what you want and need and can directly ask for what you want.

- You respect and trust yourself and demonstrate respect for others.

- You value your own ideas and opinions, while at the same time respecting the ideas and opinions of others.

- You are able to define and set limits and stick to them.

- You are confident, and you trust your own perceptions.

- You are aware of and respectful of others' boundaries.

Setting Limits: The Power of "No"

The ability to say "no" and establish limits is a hallmark of caregivers who avoid burnout and "compassion fatigue." Many of us are reluctant to set limits. In my groups and workshops, I often ask, "How many of you have a hard time setting limits?" Over 90% of the participants raise their hands every time. "How many have a hard time saying 'no'?" Same thing. I was a great "yes" person, too. Why is limit-setting difficult for some of us?

We don't want to be selfish or unkind. We want to be responsible, to fully show up for whatever is required of us, and more. For caregivers, saying "no" without feeling guilty can be difficult. Many of us are "yes" people, conditioned to be that way by our families of origin, education, and religious organizations. We were taught that we must always put others first, that our needs were not important, and, in fact, that we were selfish if we said "yes" to ourselves and "no" to others. We were taught to be agreeable, obedient, and compliant. We had great caretaker training. Some of us were shamed if we took strong stands for ourselves or asserted our powerful voices.

Because children need love and acceptance as much as they need food, safety, and shelter, they ultimately abandon their own desires and needs, at least to some extent, in order to be loved and accepted. Then, as adults, when we're faced with situations where we have to decide whether or not to say "yes" or "no" to another's needs or demands, we often automatically choose what is familiar and what we hope will avoid conflict and discomfort. We try not to rock the boat. Saying "no" can most definitely disrupt the status quo. It is much easier, we think, not to ruffle feathers. At what cost, though?

Unreservedly saying "yes" to others means you're saying "no" to your own wants and needs. If you have trouble saying "no," it's likely that you are unaware that you even have needs or what these needs are. Even if you do have this awareness, you all too quickly put these needs aside in favor of the care recipient's needs. If you are saying "yes" to another because, perhaps, you're afraid of the consequences of saying "no" and it is not an authentic "yes," you are saying "no" to you, and you are inflicting pain upon yourself. You're denying yourself. You're not acting on your own behalf. You suffer every time you abandon yourself in this way. Your unrecognized needs can start showing up in the form of physical and/or emotional symptoms: fatigue, irritability, problems with sleep, anxiety, or feelings of depression. Balancing compassion and generosity with a willingness to honor yourself and what you need will help you survive and thrive in your caregiving.

A participant in one of my workshops stood up proudly when we were talking about "the power of no" and proclaimed that, as scared as she was to do it, she had started setting limits with her father. "I got to the point where it was either him or me. I felt like I was getting sucked into his fear and unresolved anger. I was afraid of his negative reactions to me if I established more boundaries with him. I was also afraid that if I pulled back and was less available to him, that he'd sink further into his pain. I realized that I had been trying to save him from himself. Then I saw that saving him wasn't up to me. It was terrifying to see all of this, but my therapist helped me every step of the way. I was amazed that my father did not fall deeper into the abyss when I spent less time with him; in fact, he actually started to improve. He decided he needed to get some help. That's the first time I ever heard him utter those words."

If you are a friend or family caregiver, providing care can easily become a full-time endeavor. This is truly the to-do list that never ends. If your care recipient doesn't have a reliable support system with a number of people sharing in the responsibilities of caregiving, the burden can be great. As a caregiver, if you don't set limits, burn-out is almost inevitable. Once you experience burnout, or reach the point where you are depleted, exhausted, or possibly sick yourself, you are of little or no help to those who depend on you for their care. It is essential that you learn to say "no" for your own health and well-being and for the sake of those you care about.

Saying "no," for example, to doing something that your care recipients can clearly do for themselves, like preparing part of a simple meal, can empower them. If you are available for every request and preference rather than for legitimate needs, you are depriving this person of cultivating their strength, independence, autonomy, and self-confidence. In addition, saying "no" also means saying "yes." What are you saying "yes" to? You're saying "yes" to yourself. Perhaps, you are giving yourself time to exercise, to read a couple of the magazines that are piled high on your nightstand, write in your journal, or read the book you've been carrying around for days, telling yourself, "I'll get to it when I have a little time."

Jerry's wife, debilitated from four months of chemotherapy and radiation treatments, had become dependent on her husband's unfailing attention and generosity throughout the course of treatments. He was starting to experience what has come to be known as "compassion fatigue." He was anxious, irritable, exhausted, and not sleeping well. He opened up in one of the Soul Care for Caregivers workshops and revealed how terrified he was to take any time off from attending to Linda, his wife. "This is such an important time for her," he said, his voice cracking, as he tried to hold back tears. "I'm afraid she won't recover in the ways she needs to if I'm not on top of everything." No one could do the caregiving as well as he could. Jerry was afraid to delegate even though friends and family offered to help. "No one knows Linda like I do," he said. "It's hard for her to ask for what she needs. You have to be able to read between the lines." Linda had two friends who repeatedly offered to help out in any ways that she and Jerry needed. He would let them step in for brief periods but was never relaxed about it, calling regularly to "see how everyone was doing."

Hearing from others in the workshop who were facing similar dilemmas and who, Jerry could see, were suffering from "compassion fatigue," moved Jerry to take some risks. He spoke openly and honestly to Linda's friends and let them know that he really needed their help. He let himself be very vulnerable with Joan, Linda's closest friend, and told her how difficult it was for him to let go and trust anyone else to be involved with Linda's care. "I feel so much better," he said later. "My secrets are out of the bag, and I'm finally admitting that I can't do this alone. What a relief. I think this is going to serve everyone."

Another boundaries issue has to do with our investment in the health and happiness of our care recipients. Of course, we want that for them. Of course, we deeply wish that their pain would lessen or that they'd regain their strength. But there's a fine line between wanting something and being attached to whether or not it happens. It is easy to impose our expectations for another person's well-being onto that person, and in so doing, we are not fully present to them or to the reality of their situation. How do we have our preferences and hopes and, at the same time, accept the current reality? Our images of how they could or should be can keep us from simply accepting how they are. This attachment can lead to our being controlling and intrusive. We desperately want them to get better, so we get over-involved. We try to do everything we can, believing it is in their best interest. We are too vigilant about tracking their progress, watching and questioning to see if they're adhering to their medical protocols, eating properly, getting the right amount of rest, and obeying doctors' orders. We can't get our care receivers out of our minds. We feel happier and more relaxed when they have a good day, disturbed and stressed when they are struggling. Our own well-being becomes dependent on how they are doing. In addition, when things don't go as we expect them to, we may become resentful or angry, blaming ourselves, our care recipients, or other care providers.

Excessive focus on the care receiver can be a way to deflect attention away from ourselves and our own discomfort. We may be sad or frightened, perhaps feeling powerless, because we cannot do more, because there are limits to what we can control. Rather than face our feelings, we anxiously focus on the people in our care, attempting to fix them, to make things right or better, to find ways to improve this difficult situation.

Gerard's partner, Bret, had AIDS. "I couldn't leave him alone," said Gerard. "Everyone was telling me that I needed to back off, but I just couldn't. I couldn't bear to watch him wasting away in front of my eyes. When I wasn't by his side, reading to him, serving him his favorite foods, adjusting his bedding, telling him funny stories, I was on the internet, the phone, talking to everyone I knew about every alternative treatment available: what worked for whom, how reliable the source was, what the costs were, how I could find out more, on and on. Anytime I heard about anything that might help, I was on it. I couldn't sleep, was always restless and agitated. He was constantly on my mind. Bret's good friend, Marie, insisted I go to her place to have lunch with her, and she woke me up to what was at the root of the compulsive quality of my caring. "Gerard," she said. "Do you ever stop and connect with your feelings? I don't see you doing that. Will you do that right now? Will you calm down for awhile with me and see what's really going on under all your frenzy?"

Gerard went on. "I cracked. I started sobbing on Marie's couch, crying more than I'd ever cried in my life. Oh my God, I thought, this is what I've been running from. I'm devastated that I'm going to lose Bret. I haven't wanted to face the fact that I am going to lose him, that we all are. I can't stand seeing him getting weaker and weaker every day, exhausted. I can't stand the weight loss, headaches, chills, night sweats. He's such a good person. He shouldn't be dying. And he shouldn't be dying in this terrible way. He doesn't deserve this! And I don't either."

After Gerard had this emotional breakdown, which proved to be a breakthrough, he started to change. He continued to cry a lot, but he also became lighter and less frenetic. He wasn't as compulsive in his caring, hovering less around Bret, letting others step in, taking more time for himself, and not being so obsessive about seeking out cures. In addition, his contact with Bret was more intimate, which served both of them very well. Less controlling, more relaxed and present, Gerard later said that he and Bret had opened their hearts to each other in ways they never had before. "I'm letting go," he said, wistfully. "I'm facing the truth, and I've stopped trying to impose my will on everything. I'm a kinder, gentler person. I'm starting to like this new me."

Guidelines for Setting Healthy Boundaries

Here are nine suggestions to help you develop healthy boundaries:

1. Identify your goals with regard to creating healthy boundaries. What new behaviors do you want to establish? In what situations and with what people do you want to improve your boundaries? Write about why you want to make these changes. How will your caregiving be positively impacted by these changes? What fears or concerns do you have? What could get in the way of making these changes?

2. Cultivate self-awareness when you're in the presence of others. Get to know how you feel when you are connected to yourself and centered. What is your experience in your body? What are you feeling? What are your thoughts? Ask yourself questions, such as am I overly invested in the outcome of this treatment? Do I feel like I need to fix or rescue this person? Are my questions intrusive? Am I leaning in too much? Am I merging with my care receiver? Why do I feel like withdrawing? Are my walls up? Am I being too distant? What do I need to do in this moment to have a healthy boundary with this person?

3. Start small. Create small goals initially, goals that are realistic and attainable. If you want to let down some of your walls, start with people that you feel safe with. If you want to practice saying "no," begin with small items, and practice this in situations where you feel safe. Then gradually work up to more difficult challenges. It will be easier to leap

over larger hurdles after you've demonstrated some success in establishing boundaries. Defining boundaries will then become familiar, a way of being that is natural to you.

4. Whenever possible, choose to have these conversations at times when both you and your care receiver are more likely to be receptive. For example, after she has had a nap or a good meal, or when you are feeling clear and balanced. Both of you are likely to be more responsive rather than reactive if you choose your time wisely.

5. Be clear, calm, and firm when you set limits. Keep it simple; elaborate explanations or justifications are usually unnecessary. Be specific when that's appropriate. You may need to remind yourself that it's okay, in fact, necessary, to establish boundaries and that you have the right to do that.

   Imagery rehearsal is helpful here. When possible, take five to eight minutes twice a day for at least two days before your boundary-setting conversation. Imagine that you are sitting with this person and clearly and firmly saying what needs to be said. See and experience yourself as steady, calm, and clear, regardless of the person's reactions. Hear the sound of your voice. Experience yourself as grounded, feet planted firmly on the floor, with good posture, and making eye contact. Imagine this as vividly as possible and experience it in your whole body-mind.

6. Allow for the care receiver's response. You may be met with resistance, frustration, or anger. Be

prepared to respond to these reactions without being defensive. Remain firm, yet give them room to have their reactions and feelings if they're not comfortable with or in agreement with your limits. Learning how to tolerate resistance and frustration from others is an important muscle for you to develop as a caregiver.

7. If setting limits is relatively new and unfamiliar to you, it may be uncomfortable for awhile. You may feel awkward. You may uncover the fact that you are afraid of rejection, for example, "She won't like me anymore because I'm not as agreeable as I have been." You may feel guilty, concerned about being self-centered, or worried that you'll be abandoning your care receiver and harming them in some way. You may think that awful things will occur if you make this change. You're afraid that you're letting them down. These thoughts and feelings will dissipate over time. Like any new skill or behavior, the more you do it, the easier it becomes. Focus on the fact that setting boundaries is good for your care receiver, as well as for you.

8. You can use imagery to create boundaries. You might imagine a fence or a transparent, flexible shield that separates you from another person. Samantha, a drug and alcohol counselor, came up with the creative idea of imagining that she was holding up a mirror that was facing her clients whenever they'd become critical or verbally attacked her. "I just see their hostility bouncing off of me, then going back to them, not as anger, but just as energy. I used to take everything personally and criticism would really get to me. Now, most of

the time, when I remember to hold up my imaginary mirror, I'm like Teflon—nothing sticks."

9. If you encounter deep, unresolved psychological issues, get professional help. You may find that you need to work with a psychotherapist or skilled professional for a while to help you work through unhealed places in your psyche. Old wounds may become activated when you do this work, and this may be a good opportunity to do more of your own healing.

EXERCISES AND ACTIVITIES

Writing Exercise—Inquiry and Reflection

1. Write about a boundary you set recently with regard to your caregiving. What led to your establishing this boundary? How did you feel before and after setting the boundary? Is there anything you would have done differently? What did you learn?

2. What are some boundaries that you need to set? Be specific.

3. What could get in the way of your defining these limits?

4. What might your experience be if you don't set these boundaries? What if you do set them?

5. How would you describe yourself with regard to boundaries? What is easy for you? What is most

difficult? What are your strengths in this regard? Where do you see room for improvement?

6. What changes would you like to see in yourself in the coming days and weeks? Within one month? Three months? Six months? One year? Set clear and manageable goals.

7. What short and long term action steps are you willing to take to achieve your goals?

8. What could get in the way of your following through on these action items?

Writing Exercise—Ideal Boundaries

1. Choose one person with whom you are having boundary problems. Describe this situation in as much detail as possible. What does it look like? What occurs? How do you feel when you're with this person and the boundaries don't feel good to you? What do you experience in your body? How do you typically react?

2. Describe your ideal boundaries with this person. What does this look like? What are you doing, or not doing? How do you feel? What are the sensations in your body?

3. Ask yourself what you can do to improve this situation for yourself. Focus on changes that you can make, not on what you want or expect the other person to do. Your list might include items, such as "I can be honest with this person about the impact of their boundaries on me

without blaming them. I can clearly assert or ask
for what I need, etc."

4. Create action steps based on the list of changes you
    can make. What will you do and when? Be as spe-
    cific as possible.

Chapter 4

CREATIVITY IS GOOD MEDICINE: CREATIVITY AND THE CAREGIVER

Why creativity? What does creativity have to do with caregiving? I believe it has everything to do with caregiving. We carefully tend to the bodies, hearts, minds, and souls of those in our care. We deal with family members and friends of our care recipients and with health care practitioners, pharmacies, insurance representatives, lawyers, social service agencies, and many other people and institutions. As caregivers, we give a lot. We're ever on the lookout for the cracks that need filling, the voices that need to be patiently heard without judgment, and the hearts that need holding, free of our personal agendas. We tend to the everyday, the nuts and bolts of schedules, transportation, personal care, medication supervision, insurance, and legal issues. We also give our attention to the emotional world of our care receivers and their family and friends, frequently encountering fear, anger, frustration, hopelessness, and despair.

Juggling all these domains, we give the best and the most of ourselves.

You must replenish your own life force. If your well is empty, what do you have to give? However, if your well is full, the streaming life energy flowing to you and through you can invigorate everyone around you who is open to receiving your life-giving energies.

The creative force is the life force that streams through your being. Tapping into that effervescent flow at the core of your being is a way to revitalize yourself and awaken your passion for life. When you move into this current, you can express these energies in the form of paintings, essays, songs, or, perhaps, new possibilities for solving problems. You develop innovative presentations or turn nondescript backyards into magical gardens. You become vital and affirmative toward life, for you are bringing something new into being. In awakening to creativity, you awaken to the life within and all around you. You see options you may not have been seen before. What may have appeared to be a box you were trapped in becomes a field of greater possibilities. Poetry therapist James Leedy says, "Creativity builds on the innate facet of every person's inheritance, Eros, the will to live." Since caregiving can be so physically and emotionally demanding, you need as many avenues as possible to access your aliveness and life force.

I've been a creativity crusader since graduate school in the mid 1980's. As a Master's Degree project, I designed a process that I called The Transformational Writing Process that integrated guided imagery with writing. The process proved to have benefits that I didn't originally intend. I conceived of it as a transformational tool for psychospiritual development, a process for healing emotional wounds, but I didn't realize that, in addition to its being an aid for healing the psyche, people would tap into their creative abilities. They were writing poems, short stories, fairy tales, and imaginative essays. As their creativity unfolded, I watched person after person come alive in ways I hadn't seen before. I led fellow students, some faculty members, friends and friends of friends through the process to test its viability as a transformational tool. My own experience had taught me how guided imagery, writing, drawing, and making crafts were profoundly healing to my body, mind, and spirit, but I didn't fully realize how universal this might be.

A couple of years later, after much research and many more personal and professional experiences with the transformational nature of the creative process, I formed groups called Writing from the Soul and Creativity and Awakening that I continue to facilitate today. I also began developing and presenting courses on creativity in the university where I was teaching: The Psychology of Creativity, Creativity and Transformation, and Creativity and Intuition. With these mature students who were between twenty and fifty-years-old, I repeatedly witnessed dramatic changes that were brought about by the creative process.

In these classes, one of the course assignments is to present a creative project at the end of the term. I'm inspired every time I see their presentations. The students cook and bring in tasty goodies to share with the class, take nature photographs, create herb gardens, make collages, design and craft jewelry, sing—often in front of a group—for the first time since they were children, try their hand at watercolor, create dream journals, knit, quilt, and play musical instruments. They are never evaluated on the end product for they have been encouraged from the first class to engage in the process and not worry about the end result. I ask them to talk about their process on the day of their presentation and share with the class what they learned about themselves and creativity.

They talk about how they found their joy, discovered a way to connect with themselves more deeply, and found ways to become centered and balanced. They share about how creativity is helping them get through school more easily and manage stress in their lives. Some of them cry because they are coming out of hiding with a gift or a talent they've put on hold or, perhaps, haven't been willing to share with others before. Some of the adult students in this psychology program are already in the helping field, as drug/alcohol treatment counselors, somatic practitioners, coaches, nutritional counselors, nurses' aides, and employees in social service agencies and nonprofit organizations. They speak about how they are bringing or intend to bring their passion about creativity into their work as helpers. "If owning my creativity does this for me," said Bruce, a life coach, "I can only imagine how this will help my clients."

In my Soul Care for Caregivers workshops, I include a section on creativity. After a discussion about creativity and caregiving, participants create a collage using magazines, poster board, scissors, and glue with the aim of mapping their way to a creative goal. I recommend that they depict an obstacle on their collages, as well, which they know they will need to overcome. Goals have included taking a ceramics class, redecorating the bedroom, or starting a journal. The most common obstacles for these caregivers have been the belief that either they're not creative, they don't have enough time, or they're too tired for anything extra. They share their collages in small groups and support each other in developing simple plans to achieve their creative goals. I've been so moved by their reports weeks and months later of how finding their creative voice has helped them personally and improved the quality of their caregiving. They report feeling more resilient, less reactive, calmer, and more restored. "Just fifteen to twenty minutes a day thumbing through magazines and finding pictures that inspire me, then gluing them in my journal, enlivens me and, at the same time, soothes my nerves," said Chiara, an oncology nurse.

Some of the workshop participants introduce creativity to their care recipients. Donna—elder sister and care provider for Patty, who was recovering from back surgery—encouraged her sister to take up needlework, an activity that she loved to do five years earlier. Simon got a scrapbook and scrapbook materials for his mother, and together they made an album that his mother said brought back many good memories. Jeanne and her home health care worker are going on short walks, and Jeanne is taking photographs of whatever appears beautiful to her. Lily and her daughter, Zoe, who has leukemia, are experimenting with something new in the kitchen whenever Zoe wants to do that. "I haven't seen her this happy in weeks," exclaimed Lily. "She poured chocolate syrup on strawberries and marshmallows, then made a design using pirouette cookies on the top of her concoction. You'd have thought she had created a Michelangelo sculpture."

Many people equate creativity with artistic or literary expression. When I ask them if they see themselves as creative, they often say, "No. I can't paint, write, or sing." Then, after talking to them for awhile, I learn that they have fantastic organizing skills, or they are masters of innovation in the kitchen. Ronnie, an occupational therapist, can just look at a messy, disorganized closet and quickly see how to transform it into a functional, well-organized space. Sam, a nurse, bakes whenever he has free time. He makes delicious pecan bars and melt-in-your-mouth carrot cake. People love to visit Sam! The creative force is the life force, and it can be expressed in absolutely any form.

Transformative Effects of Creative Expression

Creativity is a way to bridge the conscious and unconscious. Dipping into the mysterious regions of the unconscious mind, the writer or visual artist, for example, finds symbols and metaphors, impressions, and feelings that she then brings to the surface to express through language, shapes, or colors. When you are cooking—creating your own recipes or experimenting with spices—or redecorating your office, you aren't just using your analytical mind to come up with ideas and solutions. Ahas! come from the deeper layers of the psyche. Then, you use your conscious mind to figure out how to implement and work with the insights you've received. When you encounter the inevitable obstacles of creative projects, it is often your unconscious that provides a way to overcome the block, often when you're in the car or shower, when you least expect it. The more you create, the more you learn to move back and forth fluidly between the inner and outer worlds. Anais Nin described this as "learning to walk between one realm and the other without fear, interrelate them, and ultimately fuse them." In creating, then, you move towards wholeness.

Powerful emotions and impulses can be constructively channeled into creative avenues. "I sing my sadness," says Laura, mother of a seven-year-old boy who has brain cancer. Howard expresses his pain about his father's death in dark and moving poems that emanate from the depths of his soul. "I experience the loss more deeply when I write," he said, "but at the same time, I feel better because I'm facing and feeling the truth." To deny your deep wounds is to carry them as heavy burdens in your psyche. Expressing grief, anger, or despair in creative modalities is a safe and effective way to release and transform your pain. Joy and positive emotions can be expressed more fully, as well.

Thomas constructed a beautiful mosaic tile with a heart on it to put in his mother's yard, as a way to celebrate her five-year anniversary of being cancer free.

Creative expression has a domino effect. The benefits of creativity spill over into other areas of your life. If you paint miniature figures, you are cultivating focus and presence and will find that you're more present and focused when you're performing other tasks. If journal writing is helping you to become reflective and self-aware, you'll find yourself more attuned to your inner world throughout the day. If you sew or quilt, playing with multi-colored fabrics with varied patterns enhances your visual and kinesthetic sensory awareness. The world looks more vibrant to you. Your appreciation of colors, shapes, and textures is enhanced. I once took an improv class and discovered that I became more spontaneous when I was teaching.

Spirituality and creativity are closely linked. When you engage in creative activities, you expand your consciousness. You move beyond habitual thought and behavior patterns and open up to possibilities not normally within your reach. In peak moments, you let go of control and surrender to the creative process. At times, you will enter a flow state where perceptions of time and space are altered. When fully absorbed in activities, such as sailing, dancing, playing the piano, or writing, you will forget yourself and, often, your surroundings. As your egoic self disappears, your deeper self appears. Many of the caregivers that I know who are exploring their creativity have made comments that depict the links between spirituality and creativity. Sue, a physical therapist, said, "I'm not living out of my head these days. If I'm tangled up in thoughts when I'm creating a new soup, I inevitably add too much salt or too little of something else. I'm learning to get out of the way and let the soup tell me what IT wants." Clark, a nutritional counselor, shared that taking photographs is helping him become more intimate with nature. "At first, it was only when I was looking through the lens that I could see the beauty in a single twig, in the smallest of things," he said. "Now I don't need the camera to "see the world in a grain of sand." Akemi, caregiver for her aunt who was recovering from hip surgery, reported, "When I paint, I tap into a feeling of joy I'd forgotten was there. I feel lighter, and it's gotten easier to bounce back when I've had a hard day."

The "Bright Shadow"

Unfortunately, for many of us in this culture, the limitless possibilities for creative expression that reside within us are repressed. We are a thinking culture, valuing reason and logic over feelings, creativity, and intuition. We are quick to judge people who exhibit what we label irrational behavior; we mistrust people who don't contain their feelings in the ways we deem appropriate. We don't mind watching outrageous behavior on TV or in movies, but most people don't want to bring that home. We pride ourselves on having good minds and strong intellects, but mental acuity is only one aspect of humanness. We have an unlimited and often unexpressed potential for spontaneity and imagination. For many of us, our creative gifts reside as buried treasures in the deep oceans of our psyches.

Psychiatrist Carl G. Jung coined the psychological concept of the "shadow" to describe the unacceptable and disowned parts of ourselves, the dark side of human nature. In addition to primal wounding, trauma, and instinctual drives, the shadow also holds our repressed light. The "bright shadow" is the reservoir that contains our deepest potentials, which are often relegated to the unconscious dimension of the psyche. Abraham Maslow, a pioneer in the field of Transpersonal Psychology, said, "We fear our highest possibilities." The "bright shadow" represents our disowned talents and strengths, our rich possibilities for wisdom, creative expression, and spiritual freedom. Many of us repress our gifts as much or more than we do our dark sides. A psychiatrist friend told me that his patients were more afraid of their light than their darkness. Robert Desoille called this tendency to disown our light, "the repression of the sublime." Excavating and reclaiming these untapped resources is a path to well-being.

How does creativity become repressed? You gleefully cover your face, arms, and legs with poster paint when the kindergarten teacher turns her back, and you are reprimanded for making such a mess. You're six years old, and your cow is red and yellow with an extra tail and a moustache. Your precious drawing is singled out, and you are presented in front of the class as an example of what not to do.

Francesca, a nurse's aide, recently joined a poetry group because, as she said, "I've always been a poet at heart. Everyone thought that being a poet was too weird, though, and I was repeatedly told that I could never make money writing or in the arts, so I locked my passion away." She recounted an experience she had when she was in the third grade that she said marked the beginning of when she closed the door on her creativity. "Our homework assignment was to write a story about something or someone that was important to us. My story was entitled 'Harry, the Laughing Dog.' Harry, my favorite creature in the whole world, had what looked like a perpetual smile on his face. We all joked about how we had a laughing dog. So, I wrote a story about Harry and eagerly raised my hand to be the first to read my story out loud to the class and Mrs. Craig. Well, I was about three sentences into the story when Mrs. Craig slammed a book down on her wooden desk and told me to sit down. 'Dogs do not laugh!' she bellowed with derision. 'When you go home, write a story that makes sense.'" Francesca, of course, felt humiliated. "That one experience had a profound effect on me," she said. "And I still remember it as if it happened yesterday."

Versions of Francesca's story are not uncommon. Our innocent attempts at self-expression in our formative years were implicitly or explicitly stifled. We repeatedly received messages from parents, relatives, and teachers to turn down the volume on our excitement and passion, to obey the rules, to follow directions carefully. In order to gain love and avoid disapproval, we learned to be good, to stifle our imagination and our uniqueness in order to fit in, to be proper and appropriate. We colored inside the lines, learned to make perfectly sized and correctly shaped lower and upper case a's and b's, learned to only have "inside voices" inside the house. If we were girls, we stayed away from the dump trucks and fighter planes and didn't get too dirty or yell too loud. Boys learned that playing with dolls was "sissy," and they stayed out of mommy's closet even though they may have yearned to dress up in her evening clothes and high heels. We were told that we were "too big for our britches," too intense, or, perhaps, too sensitive. The wild, strange, and foolish parts of us weren't socially acceptable, especially after a certain age. Since we needed love as much as we needed food and shelter, we slowly, but surely, disconnected from our unacceptable attributes and unconsciously locked them in a dark closet.

Sam, age six, Sophie, age four, and Sadie, age two, are my three grandchildren, and I've designated myself as their creative muse. I scrupulously avoid having them create anything that's too formulaic, like "Here's a cut-out of a snowman. You put the eyes here, and the nose and hat go there. Let's draw trees, and here's what trees should look like." I never give them coloring books because they get into thinking they have to draw inside the lines. Actually, I did give them a coloring book once for the purpose of showing them how cool it is to scribble outside the lines, color with the page upside down or glue shapes all over the images. I never look quizzically at a drawing of shapes and scribbles and say, "That looks like an airplane or a frog." Never. I let them tell me about their drawing if they choose to do that. I know I'm compensating for what I think they're getting from teachers and other adults, who insist that people have two legs and two arms, that the sun and moon must be in the sky, and that only birds can have wings. I also purposely give them buckets and flower pots full of wet dirt when they come to visit just to dig around and mess themselves up. A friend told me I should get them t-shirts that say I Heart Dirt! Fortunately, my daughter is just fine with my informal creativity coaching. "Better your house than mine," she says.

My friend, Leslie, was a hospice chaplain. She tended to the needs of the dying. Tears in her eyes, she told me how often she encountered people who regretted that they didn't follow their passions enough in their lives. Many acknowledged that they were good parents, grandparents or siblings, contributed to their families and community, and met their responsibilities as best they could. But, all too often, these men and women said that they had let their lives be consumed by practicalities. They put off their dreams or discounted the importance of their creative sides. Some were simply afraid to risk, afraid to appear foolhardy once they became adults. Leslie was so affected by their end-of-life stories that she took a serious look at her own life to see where she was abandoning herself and what aspirations she had turned her back on. After much soul searching, she decided to change careers and moved from California to New York to fulfill her long-buried desire to pursue her love of acting.

Certainly, most of us don't have the luxury of being able to pack our bags and move across the country to pursue a dream. In some instances, though, that's exactly what's called for. If you are a family or friend caregiver, that's unlikely to be an option. But Leslie's experience of encountering person after person who regretted not following their dreams points to the importance of taking these stirrings in our hearts, bodies, and minds seriously so that we don't come to the end of our lives having wished we'd followed a different course.

Devoting time and energy to creative endeavors can seem self-indulgent for caregivers who are reluctant to take time out for themselves. I attended an author event at a local bookstore, and the presenter was extolling the healing benefits of writing. A woman raised her hand and said, "I know there's truth in what you're saying. I used to write a lot before Ryan became ill. Not a day went by that I didn't write in my journal. Now, with two other kids, practically every minute of the day is taken up with parenting. The only "me" time I have is when they're sleeping, and then, I'm too tired to do anything but go to bed myself." "I know exactly what you mean," said the presenter. "My husband has multiple sclerosis, and we have two small children. There have been periods the last couple of years when it seemed truly impossible to manage it all. In those times, I wrote twice as much."

Reflecting on the specific benefits of creative expression can offset the tendency to devalue creativity and treat creative activities as just one more item on the to-do list—usually the last item on the list. Because creativity is still considered to be frivolous in many quarters—things we do only when everything else has been handled—it helps to remember why and how creativity is important and can actually help us do everything better. When you do make a commitment to include creativity in your life, you're not just confronting, for example, the inner voice that would have you focus on your caregiving night and day, but you're standing up to the collective voices we've all internalized that devalue creativity in favor of practicality, reason, and logic. We know how empowering it is to take a stand for ourselves, to say "no" to the inner and outer voices that would have us squelch our passions and say "yes" to the truths in our hearts. This is an opportunity to say, "Yes!" to that, which will bring joy, aliveness, and spontaneity into your life.

Here are 6 Tips for Awakening Your Creativity:

1. Be true to yourself. What is stirring deep in your soul that wants to be expressed? Imagine putting all the shoulds and reasons you can't follow your heart's desires into a box for now, and ask yourself, "How would I like to express my creativity? Where will I find my joy and aliveness?" Jot down whatever comes to you, and then decide to take the next step.

2. Set a clear intention. In declaring an intention, you are moving your idea from the background to the foreground of your life. Through this conscious choice, you are engaging your will to align with your vision. A clear intention is very powerful; it will set your plan into motion. Renew your intention often. It will help you stay on track and keep creative expression as a priority in your life.

3. Take risks. The egoic mind will try to convince you that danger awaits if you rock the boat in your life. The ego thrives on predictability and safety, on preserving the status quo. Your soul wants you to fly, though—to be Big and Colorful, perhaps Wild and Weird. Your soul knows you will become empowered if you take chances and break free of old habits and patterns. Say "No!" to the voice that would have you stay in your comfort zone and "Yes!" to the voice that encourages you to be all that you can be.

4. Allow for fear and uncertainty. There's nothing to fear about fear. It is natural. When you mobilize creativity, you are stepping away from the familiar and into the unknown. You are letting go of control and moving beyond the confines of your linear mind. In addition to being exciting, that can also be unnerving. Let the fear be present; acknowledge it rather than push it away or make it wrong, and move ahead with your project. Imagine giving your fear a chair to sit on right outside your door and give it something to do while you immerse yourself in your creativity. By doing that, you're respecting its presence, but not letting it inhibit your creative process.

5. Embrace the unknown. Venturing into the unknown is at the heart of creativity. We like to know what's going on, what's next, what the outcome will be. In writing this book, I fairly regularly came up to the edge of uncertainty. How shall I proceed? What shall I do next? What's needed in this section? I would fret and worry, scrambling about in my mind to figure out what to do. I stopped lis-

tening to my anxious thoughts and simply asked my intuition, "What is right action for me now?" I often heard that I needed to take a break and do something different, like go for a walk. Sometimes, my sense was that I just needed to be patient and sit with the discomfort of "not knowing" until the next step presented itself naturally. That wasn't necessarily what I wanted to hear, but the creative process doesn't work in service of the ego.

6. See your mistakes as teachers. Perfectionism is a powerful saboteur of creativity and is at the root of many creative blocks. Like fear, mistakes are inevitable and are a natural part of the creative process, which involves experimentation and a lot of trial and error. We learn from mistakes; they often lead us to new ideas and possibilities. As James Joyce said, "Mistakes are the portals of discovery."

EXERCISES AND ACTIVITIES

Writing Exercise—Your Creative Spirit: Then and Now

Answer the following questions as a way to explore your relationship to creativity and as a tool to help you take your next creative steps:

1. What does creativity mean to you? What are your beliefs about creativity?

2. What messages did you receive from childhood through adolescence from family members, peers,

teachers, and any others about creativity and, in particular, about your creativity? Take time to reflect on this question, letting your memory take you back through the years. Particular people or events may come into your awareness. Jot down everything that comes to you.

3. Who encouraged your creativity? What did this person or people convey to you?

4. Who discouraged your creativity? What did this person or people convey to you?

5. Who are your creative heroes and heroines? What specifically do you admire about these people? Assuming it was possible that each one of these people was expressing qualities that are potentials within you, what are these potentials?

6. What steps can you take to develop these potentials in yourself?

7. What are your creative dreams?

8. What are your creative fears?

9. What behaviors are keeping you from having time for creative activities, for example, watching TV or playing computer games? Write about each of these and see if you are ready and willing to commit to spending a little less time with one of these behaviors.

10. Complete the following sentences, taking five minutes for each one. Keep your hand moving and don't think about the answers.

What I would love to do is_____
What's keeping me from_____
is_____
What I can do to overcome this obstacle
is_____
I commit to_____
My next step is_____
I will know that I've achieved my
goal when_____

11. How might the quality of your caregiving be
enhanced if you included time for creative
expression?

Self-Guided Imagery Exercise— Meet Your Creative Selves

"Each of us is a crowd," writes Psychosynthesis therapist, Piero Ferrucci, in his book *What We May Be*. He is referring to the idea that our personalities are comprised of many different parts, called subpersonalities. We express different aspects of ourselves at different times. You may express the gentle, compassionate part of yourself when you are tending to your care recipient's emotional or physical pain, another part emerges when you're having dinner with a trusted friend, another with your relatives at family gatherings. Each of these semi-autonomous selves has a style and motivation of its own. The poet Fernando Pessoa writes, "In every corner of my soul, there is an altar to a different god."

You have many creative potentials—some are obvious and some are hidden—awaiting your attention. Perhaps you have a writer, violin player, sculptor, or gardener waiting in the wings to be acknowledged and invited into your life. Working with these creative subpersonalities is a way to bring them to life. I suggest that people cultivate relationships with their creative selves as they do with friends. Make regular contact, ask meaningful questions, be open, honest, and direct, and follow their suggestions if the advice sounds reasonable to you. Each of us is a crowd, and within that crowd are artists, chefs, poets, and jazz singers. Who is waiting to meet you?

Try This Creative Subpersonality Exercise:

1. Choose a creative part of yourself that you would like to develop.

2. Find a comfortable place to sit, taking a minute or so to settle in and adjust your position in any ways that you need to. When you are ready, close your eyes. Let your breathing be easy and natural. Allow the breath to move into any areas of tightness in your body. Feel yourself relaxing more and more deeply with each outgoing breath. Relax and be with your breathing like this for two or three minutes.

3. With your eyes closed, imagine an ideal environment in which to meet this creative part of you. This could be a natural setting, your living room, an office, or, perhaps, a studio. Imagine a place for you and your subpersonality to sit comfortably.

4. Let an image that represents your creative self emerge spontaneously. It could be a woman, man, object, or symbol. For example, your inner writer might appear to you as a man or woman sitting at a writing desk or, perhaps, as an aspect of nature,

like a redwood tree or running brook. Accept the first image that comes to you.

5. Let the image have a voice and express itself. Follow your natural inclinations and ask any questions that are meaningful to you, such as: What is your name? What is your purpose in my life? How can I integrate you into my life? What do you need from me? How will my caregiving be enhanced if I begin to include you more in my life?

6. Then, open your eyes, and record your meeting and conversation. You can meet with your creative self anytime that you want. Bring any and all questions. Like a friend, the more interest and care that you bring to this part of yourself, the more you will receive in return.

Chapter 5

THE VOICE OF YOUR SOUL: INTUITION AND CAREGIVING

Just as I include a section on creativity in my caregiving workshops, I also include one on intuition. Creativity and intuition are closely related. They both represent rich inner potentials available to each and every one of us. Joy, aliveness, spontaneity, wisdom, and clarity become available to us as a result of developing these natural gifts. Our caregiving is greatly enhanced, and we become happier and more fulfilled in our personal lives.

As caregivers, we're always dealing with a lot of questions. How can I best serve this person? How shall I handle the care recipient's fears? What is needed in this moment? How can I keep all these balls in the air? What is keeping me from feeling compassionate? What is right action in terms of communicating with family members? What is most important for my self-care?

I'm a champion of intuition. I like to teach people that intuition is one of their closest, most valued allies.

"Intuition is the way your soul communicates to you and guides you," I say. Like your soul, the essence of who you are, intuition is available at all times, no matter how you're feeling, where you are, or what you are doing. Your true nature *is* this boundless wisdom.

My trust in intuition has helped me get through many difficult patches in my caregiving experiences and still serves me every day. Because writing is one of the ways I access my inner wisdom, I carry a small notebook with me and frequently take it out when I need some soul guidance.

I was in the waiting room at the Endoscopy Center waiting for the results of Heidi's fourth colonoscopy. I was particularly concerned this time because she had ended up in the emergency room, just a few days earlier, with a level of abdominal pain I hadn't witnessed before. I was scared. She'd escaped having to take steroids to this point since the medication she was taking had been, for the most part, effective in managing her symptoms. She had heard and read about the side effects of steroids and told me that under no circumstances would she take "those drugs." So I was sitting there worried that this might be the time that we'd find out that no other medication would do the trick. I also couldn't let go of the recent memories of her whimpering, crying, and screaming in the emergency room from the unremitting pain. Heidi can be quite stoic, so when she cries, there is really something serious going on.

Rather than sit and stew in my fear, I decided to turn to my intuition for help. I wrote a Soul Letter and asked for guidance. "Dear Susanne," wrote my inner wisdom, "Let your shoulders drop, unclench your fists, and take five or six deep breaths right now. That will help you relax. You are very tense." I did that, and what happened when I let go was that I felt how sad I was that Heidi had to endure all of this pain, and that she could possibly have more discomfort ahead of her. "You have a lot of feelings that just need to be acknowledged right now. The trip to the emergency room and today's procedure have been hard for both of you."

This may sound obvious, or just like common sense, but it was information I wasn't able to access just by listening to my thoughts. I put down the pen and let myself feel the sadness that was sitting under all the worry and fretting. I didn't feel happy after this, but I felt connected to myself in the moment, and the anxiety dissipated.

In each moment, you have an opportunity and a choice to be led either by the voice of inner wisdom or by the familiar aggregates of thoughts, beliefs, feelings, and images which comprise our personalities. Will fear direct you when you choose where to live, or will joy? Will a longing for the abatement of loneliness determine your choice of a partner, or will you choose who to love because they will further your growth, and you theirs, in healthy ways? Do you decide to take another computer course rather than piano lessons because it's in your heart to do so or because your practical mind convinced you that it's the more "reasonable" thing to do? Which voice inside of you chooses? Do your choices foster or hinder your growth? Are you acting for or against yourself and others? How do you make choices that are aligned with your soul rather than your personality? What keeps you from being able to hear, see, and feel the wise knowing that's always in the background of your awareness, waiting for you to turn towards it? How can you open the doors and windows to your intuition and then act on the knowledge that you acquire?

The word intuition comes from the Latin *intueri*, meaning to look, regard, or know from within. Intuition is a mode of direct knowing, which is outside the range of the usual five senses and is not mediated by a conscious rational process. You can know things directly without necessarily knowing how you know them.

Roberto Assagioli, MD, a psychiatrist and founder of Psychosynthesis, says that intuitive cognition is "immediate, direct, and holistic." In other words, it's an immediate grasp of a whole, something in its entirety. This is different from logical thought, which proceeds from one element to another in a sequential fashion. Intuition resides right below the surface of your conscious mind and is actually easy to access. You simply need to develop the habit of directing your attention there, have some tools on hand, and have the willingness to act on what you know.

Cultivating a capacity to tap into intuition is a way of life. By learning to slow down and fine-tune intuitive awareness, you can be in constant contact with the source of your being and have all of your choices reflect the truth of who you are. Intuition can assist you in caregiving with everything from problem solving and making treatment and other health care decisions to helping you discover the deeper meaning of the caregiving experiences in your life. As author and physicist Gary Zukav says, "Intuition is a walkie-talkie between the personality and the soul." If you let your intuition guide your decisions and actions, you develop a rooted trust in your own core. You are less likely to be pulled off center by the shifting winds around you. You stop letting externals define you and come to rely on your own wisdom and power. You develop confidence and stop giving your authority away to others.

Having more clarity and accuracy in your decision-making process, you become efficient and effective. You will have more energy—greatly needed by caregivers—because you're not struggling with yourself, trying to figure it all out in your head. You're able to read subtle cues about people, often aware of things about them they can't see themselves. You acquire deeper insights into your own patterns. Communication is enhanced because of the clarity you have about yourself and others.

In this culture, we have learned to lead with and defer to our intellects and to distrust knowledge that can't be empirically validated, such as the intuitive variety. Of course, being able to think clearly and critically serves us well. We need to be able to assess and define problems, devise strategies for dealing with them, clarify goals, examine options, and collect and analyze data. We need the powers of analysis and skillful discrimination. But many of us have become so identified with logical and rational thought that we have lost touch with the nonlinear parts of our minds, including imagination, insight, creativity, and intuition. We have come to believe that the reasoning mind is all that we are. As Buddhist meditation teacher Stephen Levine said of the rational mind: "It's a good tool, a good servant. But all too often, it becomes a terrible master."

Most children are required to have good reasons for their choices and decisions, especially when they contradict adult expectations. If I didn't feel like coming downstairs when Uncle Jimmy visited or eating the strawberry shortcake my grandmother brought to our house, I had to clearly explain why. If the reasons weren't clear and justified, my feelings and preferences were discounted. Many parents invalidate children's intuitive perceptions.

Intuitive knowing is not a substitute for reason. Nor should reason be a substitute for intuition. We need them both. Ideally, they complement each other. When I write, for example, I move back and forth between the different parts of my mind. I may have a sudden insight about an idea I want to work on. Then, I use reason to decide how to develop the theme and craft the thoughts and words in a way that makes sense and is well-integrated into the text. Even in the areas of science and medicine, it is often intuition that is responsible for an initial idea after which logic and reasoning are employed to provide validation and proof.

Albert Einstein, who said, "Imagination is more important than knowledge," described science as a process of intuitive leaps followed by backfill to experiment and test those leaps of genius, otherwise known as intuition. His General Theory of Relativity was just such an example. Einstein fashioned an intuitive hypothesis about the physical world, and science proceeded to test and prove that hypothesis.

Fortunately, it is easy to cultivate intuition, even if it has been long repressed, and you don't have to wait for hunches or spontaneous insights. Intuition is never far away. It is readily available.

However, in order to develop reliable, ongoing communication with this knowing, it's important to value this faculty. The conditioning of many years of reason training doesn't shift easily. Numerous internal and external messages still tell you this inner work is frivolous, meaningless, and even crazy. You may feel that developing intuition is a waste of time, that you'll be neglecting your important caregiving responsibilities for this pursuit. You may be warned that intuitive knowledge is invalid because it cannot be easily measured or proven. It may be challenging to confront such messages and patterns and take a strong stand for a choice that may not be understood or accepted by others. But if you do, you can move one step closer to being aligned with your essential nature.

Exploring Your Connection to Intuition

In order to fully commit to this work, it is helpful to reflect and write about what intuition means to you, your current and past experiences with intuition, and how your caregiving could benefit by having easier access to this natural way of knowing. Here are some questions for inquiry and reflection.

Begin with a few minutes of a centering activity, such as stretching, deep breathing, or meditating. Then, sit down and begin to write with an attitude of openness and curiosity. You are posing questions for reflection to your inner wisdom. Let responses come to you rather than putting effort into this process. Relax as you write. Try not to censor anything. There are no wrong answers here. Include thoughts, feelings, images, and physical sensations as you write. Spend five to ten minutes with each question.

1. What does the word intuition mean to me?

2. What messages did I receive about intuition from family, school, religion, or other sources? Be specific, and take time to reflect on each one.

3. When have I followed my inner knowing? Be specific. What were the results?

4. What were some instances in which I went against my intuition? What were the results?

5. How might my caregiving improve by trusting my inner wisdom? How might my relationship with care recipients and their family and friends, health care professionals, and others be enhanced? How might my emotional and physical health benefit by listening more closely to my intuition?

6. What are the ways I receive intuitive messages, hunches, or insights? Is this knowing in my body,

do I get "gut feelings," see images, get sparks of recognition, or do I just know things?

7. In what areas do I trust intuition the most? For example, is it with people, ideas, or the physical, material world? In what areas do I trust inner knowing the least?

8. What keeps me from trusting my intuition?

9. What other questions, ideas, or feelings does this inquiry bring up?

Cultivating and Committing To Your Intuition

If you decide that you value intuition and have a clear intention to cultivate it, an ongoing commitment is important. You need to choose this again and again because the pulls are strong to return to habitual ways of thinking and acting. As caregivers, it may seem daunting to make time for yet one more self-care practice. You will find yourself with more time and more flow when you are involved in your many tasks if you are choosing and acting from your center rather than from your head and personality.

Marguerita, a social worker with a very full caseload, has been "letting her soul take charge," as she puts it, for over a year now, and she is excited about the personal and professional changes she's experiencing. "I was always in my head," she reported. "It was like a ping pong match in there. I'd go back and forth about decisions, and not only was that stressful and tiring, but I also wasted a lot of time doing it. Then, when I did make a decision, I'd often waste more time second-guessing myself, wondering if it was the right decision. I've always prayed but never real-ized that I could have a two-way communication with my soul. Once the communication channel was opened, the messages I got were so helpful and wise that I started trust-ing them. I've discovered that no question is off limits. I ask about particular clients, challenges with colleagues, issues that come up in the agency, and everything else you can think of. I even talk to my body now, asking what it wants to eat and when, and I've lost fifteen pounds! Of course, I don't blindly act on every piece of information I get. I think things through before I act and make sure that the insights make sense to my rational mind."

In addition to making a commitment to this inner work, you need to acknowledge that this will take time. Patience is necessary, as is true with everything from plant-ing a vegetable garden to learning how to play the piano, or working on a new relationship. Expecting quick results or progress that is smooth and without difficulties will be frustrating, at best. This is a process that has a cyclical nature, like all of life's growth. There will be periods when it seems that your soul is slumbering, when you can't eas-ily find your intuitive connection. Perhaps you are ill, out of sorts, or just "off the beam," as my daughter says. At other times, you will feel as if you are surfing through the days, making all the right connections with people, find-ing just the right words when you need them, and easily making decisions that turn out to be of benefit to your-self and others. Sometimes, you simply won't know why you're not able to tune into intuition. Contemplating the popular motto from twelve-step programs—"Progress, not perfection"—can be of great help here.

A common question that comes up frequently in my lectures and classes is: How can we know if our intuition is accurate? Instead of intuition, could it be fear, aversion, or, perhaps, wishful thinking? How do I know which voice is the "real" one? These are important and difficult questions. If you are not familiar with how intuition communicates to you, this process, as mentioned earlier, will take time. It can take days, weeks, or even months to accurately distinguish the voice of intuition from the myriad other feelings and voices within you.

Also, trial and error is part of this learning. There will be both successes and failures, as with the development of any skill, until you are stabilized in your knowing. Because of this, it's a good idea to experiment with smaller issues and questions, ones that are not highly charged for you. For example, it's a good idea initially to check in with your intuition about questions you have regarding a friendship rather than questions about your caregiver relationship. If your connection with your care recipient is fraught with conflicts or other difficulties, it is a good idea to approach this issue when you are more confident with the techniques or when you have established some neutrality about the situation. If you are strongly invested in a particular outcome, it can be more difficult to see or hear clearly. It's also possible to use a technique, such as Soul Letters, to help you ascertain how you can shift to a more neutral position. You could ask your intuition how to step back from intense feelings about a situation so that you can see it more objectively.

Information that you receive needs to be checked out for its veracity whenever possible. You can experiment with all kinds of simple tests to assess the accuracy of intuition and to hone your powers of self-awareness. For example, you might try to guess what color clothing a family member will be wearing at an upcoming gathering, who is calling when the telephone rings, or how many homeruns your favorite baseball team will score. Keep a record of your guesses in a notebook.

Practice carefully tuning into your body and your feelings when you're in all kinds of situations, beginning to discern what you are picking up about people and places. Do you experience an openness in your chest or warmth in your limbs when you're in the presence of someone you like, perhaps someone you believe to be honest and kind? Begin to notice how different people affect you. What do you sense when you're in a room where there is hostility or where there is ease and laughter? Do you get any messages when you're driving, for example, where a parking place might be? Listen to your body when you go into a movie theater, asking yourself whether or not you'll like the film; then, afterwards, see if you were right or not. You can do the same thing before eating or going to visit friends or family. Whenever you get a hunch or insight, write it down. Make notes about accurate "hits," as well as hunches you ignored or found were mistaken.

How do you distinguish the voice of intuition from other internal voices? Your intuitive voice is often calm, fair-minded, and reasonable. It has a quality of equanimity and integrity. Imagine the voice of the most wise and trustworthy person that you know. Your inner wisdom may sound something like that. Your inner knowing will not judge, blame, or shame you. It doesn't sound like a critical parent. You won't feel like a child who has done something wrong. Neither is it grandiose, controlling, or manipulative. An intuitive message may be strong and direct, though. For instance, we get a strong sense that we shouldn't travel on a particular day, but our inner wisdom doesn't present the material in a way that is demanding or belittling. A lot of shoulds, finger pointing, or reprimands are most likely not coming from the intuitive self. Your soul genuinely cares about you. It is on your side, guiding you in ways that are in your best interest.

When intuition is operating, there is often a quality of relaxation, confidence, or, sometimes, aliveness. Begin to take note of your unique ways of knowing when an intuitive recognition is accurate, and look for those cues to determine the accuracy of your perceptions.

When I've asked course participants how they distinguish intuitive knowing from other ways of knowing, their responses included:

- It feels like a click. There is a sense of rightness.

- My body relaxes. My shoulders drop. Sometimes, I sigh or take a deep breath.

- True knowing comes from a deeper place than my mind.

- I feel it in my heart. There's a feeling of peacefulness.

- The voice of intuition is never harsh or judgmental.

- I suddenly feel more confident and solid in what I know.

- I get clear-headed. Then, I feel relieved. "Now, I can put that to rest," I say to myself.

You need to continually monitor and evaluate the intuitive information you receive with your powers of reason and discernment, as you would the advice received from any source. Carefully consider the information and make sure you are clear about the messages you're getting in the context of your whole range of options. Ask yourself, "Is this advice truly wise? Is it really in my best interest? Does it make sense to me? Is it reasonable?"

EXERCISES AND ACTIVITIES

Before you work with the following writing exercises and meditations, two considerations are important: first of all, be as clear as you can about the question or issues you want to explore. If it is a question, formulate it as clearly and succinctly as possible. For example, if you are a professional caregiver, your questions could be: what am I learning in my current job as a psychotherapist? Or how is my work serving my needs? How am I contributing to the lives of others? You can be even more specific, as in, how is my work serving my needs mentally? Physically? Emotionally? Spiritually? Think about what you want to know and be sure the question or phrasing of the topic reflects that. A less specific exploration could be to simply look at yourself and your current job without a specific focus. That can be all right, too, if general information is what you want.

The other guideline is to be as relaxed, neutral, and centered as you can when you direct your attention inward. This won't always be easy, especially when you approach your intuition with subjects that are emotionally charged or that are important to you. The more attached you are to the outcome, the more difficult it may be to get a clear answer. You may filter out truth if you insist on particular or positive answers to your questions. Intuitive listening works best when you are willing to see or hear what is true rather than what you want to be true. For this reason, as I mentioned earlier, it's a good idea to begin practicing these methods with less significant matters about which you feel relatively neutral until you've developed an ease and trust with the practices. To begin, meditate for a few minutes, stretch, or do any other centering exercise.

Writing Exercise—Write Choices

Use this writing practice when you are deciding between two or more options, for example, what type of physical activity is best for me right now: walking or swimming? Shall I have that boundaries conversation with my care recipient when we are alone or when her husband is in the room?

Have a separate, blank piece of paper for each option. Choose one of the possibilities to focus on, putting aside all thoughts and considerations about the others. You can imagine putting the second option on a back burner or in a contained space, like a box, until you are ready to examine it. Have the paper in front of you, close your eyes, and imagine as vividly as possible that you are making the first choice. You are not thinking about the choice here; you are feeling it, experiencing it in your body, visualizing it, perhaps. Imagine it with as much detail as possible. If the option is going for a walk, imagine that you are leaving the house and walking outside. You are either taking a familiar route or, perhaps, walking in a new area. Experience yourself walking and simply notice all that you can, without judgment or interpretation. Then, when you're ready, open your eyes and begin writing while you're still connected to the experience. Write about what you're feeling, what you see, what you sense, what you know. Don't censor the writing or attempt to analyze it. When you feel complete, take some deep breaths or get up for a couple of minutes and move around. Come back and prepare to repeat the exercise with the next option.

At times, the differences between the two choices will be clear to you. You will feel open, expansive, perhaps calm, clear, or have a sense of rightness when the choice is the right one for you. At other times, the distinction may not be as apparent. In this case, do some open-ended writing in response to each choice in order to flesh out more information. Just write whatever comes to you as you reflect on each option again. If you are still unclear, you can either repeat the exercise, come back to it at another time, or explore the question with a different technique, such as a Soul Letter.

Writing Exercise—Soul Letter

A Soul Letter is a way to dialogue with your intuition in writing. This is an exercise that I use all the time, with any and every question for which I need inner direction, help, or guidance. You will write two letters: one from you to your soul, or however you name your intuition, and one from your soul to you. Frame your questions carefully and pose them to your wisdom as if you were writing to your best friend and asking for advice. Here's an example from a participant in a workshop:

Dear Higher Power,

I'm worried about Ben today. He's pale, can't hold food down, and just wants to stay in his room. He won't talk to me about his feelings about the MRI results. I can't reach him, and I really want to help. What shall I do?
Love,
Meriam

Before you begin the second letter, which is your soul responding to you, take a few deep breaths or stretch for a minute or so. Practice learning to suspend your doubts and relax as you take dictation from your intuition. You can even give your "doubting self" a task to do, such as: "Go outside for a few minutes and think about how we're going to clean up the garage." For example, I tell people in workshops when they're doing this exercise to tell their doubts to take a break and go out together to a café for a latte. Stay present as you write, allowing the material to flow through you easily and effortlessly. You are inviting the wisdom that is naturally present just beneath the surface of the thinking mind to reveal itself to you. Don't judge or evaluate the thoughts and ideas that are coming to you as you write. Keep your focus off of results and just write.

Meriam's Higher Power responded with the following advice:

Dear Meriam,

You are trying to control the situation with Ben by getting in your head and strategizing, analyzing, trying to figure out what to *do*. Ben feels your anxiousness and your need for him to be other than how he is. You want to do something here, and the best thing you can do for Ben is calm yourself and be open-hearted when you're around him. You are fortunate in that he tells you that your "Mom fear and worry" upsets him. Practice allowing for your feelings, which you can do by writing them out, and then getting back to being calm and clear-headed. Right now, that's the best thing you can do for him. A brisk walk as soon as you can do that will help, too.

Your friend,
Higher Power

Meriam sighed deeply after this exercise and spoke about how true she knew this advice was. "How quickly I forget," she remarked. Through the writing and by directing attention away from the worrying chatter of her mind, she was able to access her natural wisdom.

Self-Guided Imagery—Paths of Knowing

This is an imagery practice that you can use in the decision-making process when you are considering options. Find a place to sit comfortably, and when you are ready, close your eyes and take a few minutes to settle in and relax. Let your shoulders drop and belly soften. Bring your attention to your breathing, simply following the sensations of the breath in your abdomen or chest as the breath comes in and goes out. Let your breathing be easy and natural. Now, imagine that you are standing at a juncture with as many paths moving out from where you are as there are options. If, for example, you are deciding between two options, such as whether to purchase a new car or keep the one you have, you will imagine a new car at the end of one path and the car you currently own at the end of the second path. You don't have to have clear visual images of the options. You might even just see the words, "new car" and "car I have now," etc. at the end of the paths. As you did in Write Choices, keep your attention fully on one possibility at a time, keeping the others out of awareness.

Next, imagine walking along one of the paths and carefully observe all of your reactions, without manipulation or judgment, as you proceed. Be aware of images, feelings, physical sensations, and auditory cues. Proceed along the path until you reach your destination—the choice of purchasing a new car, for example—and then, again, notice all of your reactions as you imagine making this choice. You are not evaluating anything yet, just noticing. When it seems right to do so, return to the juncture where you began, take a few deep breaths, center yourself, and repeat the process with the next path, following the same instructions. Always be sure to return to the juncture where the paths meet before walking along a path.

Reflect on the choices and note the differences between the experiences. No detail is unimportant. You will most likely have clarity about which option is preferable. You may also be surprised at what your deeper knowing has revealed or you may discover that you need more clarity or wish to gain additional insight about the rightness of this choice for you. If so, you can compose a Soul Letter or do the Talking to the Wise Ones self-guided imagery process.

Self-Guided Imagery—Talking to the Wise Ones

Formulate one or more questions that you would like some guidance about. Keep the question(s) in the back of your mind; then, find a comfortable place to sit for about fifteen minutes. Check in with your body, adjusting your position in any ways that you need to. Close your eyes and take a couple of minutes to sit quietly as you begin to focus your attention inwardly. Mentally scan your body, noticing any areas of tension, and gradually begin to allow relaxation to flow into those spots. Let yourself become more and more relaxed. Take a few slow, deep breaths. Now, imagine that you are going to a beautiful place in nature, perhaps a place you've been to before or one you imagine now for the first time. Explore this environment, noticing sounds, smells, colors, textures, the feel of the air on your skin, and how you feel in this place. Find a comfortable place to sit. An intuition figure, something or someone that represents wisdom to you, is going to join you in your nature sanctuary. An eagle, dolphin, redwood tree, or a wise sage may appear. This figure is a symbol of your inner wisdom and is here to guide and help you in your life. You can speak with them and ask questions as you would to a dear friend. Ask your question(s); then, open yourself to their response, which may come through words or in some other form that will be understandable to you. If you are not clear, you can ask for more clarity. Spend as much time as you like in dialogue with this symbol of your intuition, knowing that you can return to this place and have this exchange whenever you want. You can work with the same figure in the same place or a different figure in a different environment. Do what works for you.

Chapter 6

THE WRITE WAY TO WELL-BEING: HOW TO CREATE A CAREGIVER'S JOURNAL

I unknowingly discovered the transformational power of journal writing when I was fifteen. Home from school for six months with mononucleosis, I could barely lift my head from the pillow for the first three weeks. It was another month before I regained any of my life energy. As a result, I was pulled deeply into my inner world.

Marion Quigley, home tutor, diarist, and chamber musician, gave me my first diary, with lock and key. It had "Diary" printed in gold leaf on the cover. When she handed it to me, I felt like she was giving me something important and very special. When I could sit up, she encouraged me to make daily entries in which the only rule was "no censoring." "Write anything and everything that occurs to you," she said. "Anything goes." She seemed to know how much was bottled up inside me and that writing would be a healing tool. I began revealing my secrets in the small green book. Many of the writings were detailed word paintings of the turbulent inner world of an adolescent girl: Was I pretty enough to have a boyfriend? Would anyone ever want me? Why did Sandra get all the boys? I hated that I wasn't as cheery and outgoing as the cheerleaders and ached about missing out on all the fall school events because of my illness. I wrote about how scared I was that my friends would forget about me. I admitted that I liked having Mom and Dad worry about me, that I was relieved I didn't have to do chores, and that I loved having my parents and brother wait on me. At times, I'd cry and crying had never come easily to me. I grieved the death of Sweetheart, my parakeet, giving full rein to feelings I'd blithely dismissed two months earlier.

Here was a safe place that I could express anger. Anger was another feeling that I'd put the lid on for most of my fifteen years. My father used to brag to friends and family that he never heard me raise my voice or say an unkind word. Every time I heard him say that, I'd quietly cringe. "You have no idea what has been boiling inside me," I'd think. As I wrote, I discovered, for example, that I was much more upset than I thought I was about not being invited to Arlene's birthday party a few months earlier. In fact, I was seething. I wrote unabashedly about what a mean girl Arlene was, thinking about ways I could turn other girls against her. Other slights, losses, and rejections bubbled to the surface, and my dear diary heard it all. I wrote about how much I hated my math teacher, Mr. Reynolds, for being so strict and unyielding, wishing he'd get lost in the woods on one of the camping trips he was always bragging to us about and never come back to school. My diary became a place for revealing fears, hopes, and dreams that I had never fully admitted to myself.

The diary also became a place to unlock the doors of my imagination. I had glimpses of greater possibilities for my life. I wrote stories about myself as a writer, doctor, and teacher, talking to audiences about my latest book, or walking through hospital wards tending to the sick. The poet in me also came to life. For a while, I wrote a poem every day. Even though my outer world was small, confined to bed or my room due to the virus I had contracted, my inner world flourished. Writing became an ally and a practice that helped heal my body, heart, and soul.

Journals are powerful transformational tools and can be used for any purpose you can imagine. You can journal your feelings, dreams, goals, visions, daily activities, experiences, and insights about your day. You can have a career journal in which you track your successes, new ideas, challenges, and how you overcame obstacles. You can also have an ideal career journal that becomes a place for you to articulate your vision for your ideal work, plan how you will manifest your dream job, identify resources you'll need along the way, write about hurdles you may encounter, and explore strategies for overcoming them.

You may keep a spiritual journal in which you explore your relationship to your spirituality. You may write about current concerns or areas of inquiry, do intuitive writing, perhaps in the form of Soul Letters, collect quotes from people you admire, track your spiritual development, explore lessons you are learning, and identify significant shifts and turning points.

Some journals contain mostly what I call "stream writing," that is, unstructured, uncensored writing in which you simply allow whatever's inside to come out. You may want to include stories, poems, dialogues, or responses to writing exercises. Some people just maintain one journal, putting all the pieces of their lives into that one book. Others have a couple of journals for different purposes, and some have a separate journal for each area of their lives: family, relationships, work, finances, health, creativity, and spirituality. There are no rules for how many journals you should have or how you use them. All that's important is that all aspects of the journaling process feel right to you. And, of course, that can change over time.

"My journal grows me," said Cecilia, primary caregiver for her father who has Alzheimer's disease. "I tell the truth on those pages. I dig deep, past the ripples of the surface of my mind, and I dive down into the depths of my being. Sometimes, it takes awhile to get there. I often write a paragraph or two that sounds like the grocery list, but then, I relax, sink in, and find buried treasures. I'm not always comfortable with what I find when I write from this deep place. I feel like I'm opening the door to dark closets within me that I've been trying to avoid. Just yesterday, when I was writing, memories of times that Dad was active, energetic, and full of life surfaced, and I couldn't stop sobbing. I realized I'd been doing all kinds of things, like eating too much and watching a lot of TV, so that I wouldn't have to feel that sadness. The writing opened this up. It may be painful at times, but when I write like this, I always feel more connected to myself. I get to the real me, and there's something supremely satisfying about that. I feel lighter, like a weight's been lifted off of my chest."

When you write from a place of presence without censoring or "making writing happen," simply allowing what is there to be expressed, you are likely to access the mysterious regions of the unconscious mind, the repository of our memories, instincts, insights, and deepest potentials. Not only do you sometimes tap into forgotten reservoirs of pain, but you also access the light, love, and inspiration that you may be disconnected from.

Deep writing can take you to the heights and the depths. It is alive and juicy, sometimes raw. It may be surprisingly tender, or perhaps fragile. Unhampered by the constraints of the linear, thinking mind, neglected demons and angels unearth themselves and burst into the light of day.

If you want to explore these depths when you write, hold that intention even before you begin writing. While you're writing, fully let whatever is present for you in your body, mind, and feelings be expressed, and freely come through you onto the page. You may write about your frustration with your care receiver's primary physician, who isn't responding to her calls, your need for more time for yourself, or your excitement about the progress that your care receiver is making. As my home tutor said, "Anything goes." Write it all out. Allow words, feelings, images, and sensations to pour out, unhampered by reason or logic. Turn on the faucet, and let the waters of your psyche run freely. You'll be surprised at the gems in your being that will reveal themselves to you as you practice releasing control and allowing the words to flow.

What you write may not make sense at times, which is just fine. You are reaching beyond the rational mind. Choose to let the writing happen. Notice when you become distracted by sounds or sights around you or when your mind wanders toward wondering where this writing is going. Notice whether the inner critic acts up by attacking you with a flurry of belittling remarks. Acknowledge the tendencies that take you away from the moment. Give them a brief nod, and begin practicing your ability to choose to let them go, returning again and again, if need be, to the here and now. Relax your body; take some deep breaths now and then. If you find yourself thinking too much, just notice that and choose to return to your body, your feelings, to what you're experiencing in the present moment. If you notice that you are clenching your jaw or your shoulders are raised, gently release your jaw or let your shoulders drop. Relaxing and continuing to return to your emotions or sensations in your body in the present moment will soften your defenses and help you move deeper within.

A journal is a safe and secret place where anything goes. There are no shoulds, no explanations why, no thought too strange, no feeling off limit. You can be an angry child who's speaking for the first time in forty years or a poet who's been hiding in the shadows waiting to find her voice. Frozen pockets of grief concerning your care recipient's suffering may thaw and your wise inner knowing can offer insight. Writing is liberating. Writing transforms you. Writing invites the forgotten and the forbidden. When you write from your soul, forgetting about grammar, spelling, punctuation, and whether or not the writing is "good," you are bypassing the analytical mind and gaining entrance into the wild, rich, mysterious, and alive realms of the unconscious.

Writing makes you aware. When, for example, you write honestly about your job, and discover, as you write, that you are much less satisfied with your current situation than you were willing to admit, it won't be as easy from then on to deceive yourself. Writing is a powerful tool for dismantling your coping strategies and bringing you into an authentic encounter with yourself. This is both good and bad news—good because it brings you to truth, bad because it brings you to truth. As my daughter Heidi says, "The truth will set you free, but first it might make you miserable." "Writing from the soul is not news, weather, and sports," I say to the participants in my Writing from the Soul workshops and writing groups. "It will take you to places that aren't necessarily comfortable and that you might not have been prepared for. It's an exciting endeavor because of this and, at times, a scary one, too."

Because writing brings you face to face with yourself and can be a vehicle for opening up to repressed unconscious material, it is a good idea to be discerning about when you choose to do deep writing. For example, if you know on a given day that two hours after your writing period, you will be spending time with your patient or loved one and s/he may be in a particularly difficult emotional or physical state, it might be best not to delve into your unconscious that day at that time. Or it might actually be healing for you to open up to feelings that have been simmering just below the surface so that you can be more present to yourself and to your care receiver. Clearly, this will be different for everyone and will depend on a variety of conditions and circumstances. What's valuable to know and remember here is that soul writing is powerful and that your mind, body, and emotions are likely to be impacted.

In 1993, after my father died, I couldn't write in my journal for months. My feelings were just too raw, and I didn't want to bring that pain to the surface any more than I had to. I've always liked the quote from Emily Dickinson, "The truth must dazzle gradually, else all men be blind." When I did decide to spend more time with this writing about my father and his death, I wrote in small doses for a while. I balanced out the feelings of loss and sadness with my awareness of the many strengths he passed on to me that were still alive and well in my being. I wrote about his resiliency, optimism, and his unfettered loyalty to my mother and our family. Putting these positive qualities into words was uplifting. I felt empowered, and the gaping hole of his loss became easier for me to withstand. When I included both the light and the dark in my writing, I felt less despair.

If you do find that you opened to feelings that are, perhaps, too uncomfortable or overwhelming, you can always stop writing and shift your attention to a positive sensate experience, such as walking around the room and looking out the window at trees or getting up and gently stretching in ways that feel good to you. Becoming grounded in your body and bringing awareness to your senses in soothing or pleasurable ways can help reorient and stabilize you. Most important is listening to yourself and, at times, experimenting, to discover what helps and what doesn't. Don't push yourself. Honor and respect your needs.

A Caregiver's Journal is a resource for facilitating your well-being as you engage in the rewarding and challenging work of caring for others. This journal can be a place where you moan and groan about difficult family members, uncooperative patients or friends, lack of adequate resources, conflicting demands on your time, too much red tape or bureaucratic snags, and your own sense of being overwhelmed or fatigued. It can be a place of celebration of your care receiver's improvements, the cohesive and supportive team that you're working with, your renewed vitality, hurdles that you've overcome, or creative accomplishments. You can collect your own intuitive writings in the journal and turn to them when you need wise and helpful reminders. You can write prayers and meditations in your journal, gather inspirational words and images, then free write in response to them, sharing your associations, feelings, and insights. You can include "unsent letters" in your journal, which are honest and uncensored outpourings to people, which might contain uncomfortable truths that you're not willing or able to communicate in person. These unsent letters may also be expressions of the profound love or gratitude you feel that you cannot speak in person. Unsent letters are a potent tool for speaking "the unspeakable."

Your entire caregiving journey can be recorded and reflected upon in your journal. You may write about what you're learning, how you are growing as a person, how blocked or frustrated you feel, how you are or are not taking care of yourself. Your process of committing to and maintaining wellness can be explored and worked with. You might also include a section for practical matters and include short and long term goals and action steps and plans in that section. This journal can be a good place to keep track of the inner and outer resources that you need for every aspect of your caregiving experience and what you will do to garner these resources. You can have a section in which you list websites, books, articles, audios, and videos that are or could be helpful to you, both in terms of your own self-care and in terms of providing you with important information or concrete advice you may need.

In my experience, caregivers need every helpful tool and form of support they can find. A journal is inexpensive, portable and, of course, you can write in it anywhere, at any time of the day or night. If it's three in the morning, you can't sleep, and you can't call your best friend, your trusty journal is always there.

Guidelines for Creating a Caregiver's Journal

1. Select a book and writing implements that feel right to you. Again, there are no rules here. Some people do their journaling on their computers, on blogs, for example, while some simply prefer writing to typing. Some like to write on legal pads, while some "journalers" like to invest in beautiful, blank books of lined or unlined paper. The journal vehicle is often an important decision for people who are particular about their books. I only write on unlined pages with a fountain pen with black or

blue ink. You may prefer a ballpoint pen, pencil, or colored pens. Try not to compare yourself to others since there are no right tools.

2. Choose locations, times, and environmental conditions to write that, like your writing implements, feel right to you. Some people work best when they have structure and predictability with regard to this personal writing. They like to write at the same time each day and in the same place whenever possible. They like as much quiet as possible. That is fine. That may or may not be true for you. This may change over the months and years. I know people who take their journals with them and write in cafes, restaurants, at the beach, in their car, or on benches at the mall. Some folks need long blocks of time for their writing; others take out their journals while they're waiting in the doctor's office. When it comes to the personal process of journaling, whatever works for you is what is right.

3. Don't worry about grammar, punctuation, or spelling. You are not writing to publish. You are writing "to bring out all kinds of things that lie buried deep in your heart," as Anne Frank said. Editorial concerns like grammar and spelling are for your logical, analytical mind, which does a fine job with those matters. Focusing your attention on these issues can limit the possibilities that deep writing confers.

4. Consider privacy. Again, this is a very personal, but important matter. Do you care if others read your journal? Are there only particular people from whom you want to keep this material, or do you prefer that no one sees your writing? Are there only certain things that you don't want others to see?

Do you fully trust that your journal won't be read if you ask the people you live with not to read it? These are uncomfortable questions, but I think it's important to ask them. Journals are tempting to read, even if you live with people of great integrity. What is important here with regard to privacy is that you feel safe so that you can be absolutely honest in your journal. This is the place where you may be sharing your secrets. You will be open and vulnerable here. Some people choose to be "open books" in their lives, and this isn't an issue for them at all. Others fully trust that their journals won't be read by the people in their home. There are those who are wary or very protective of their privacy. If you are one of the latter, take some time to consider what you need to do to ensure privacy. An option is to have a trusted friend keep your journals; another is not to save journals at all. You can also delete or tear out sections that you never want anyone to see. You may have a good place to hide your journals or a way to lock them up. Do whatever you need to do so that you can feel free and uninhibited when you write.

5. Include pictures, drawings, and/or doodles if you like. I love to make mini-collages and put them on some of the blank pages in my journals. I write all around the pictures, and the combination of words and images is very satisfying for me. Cutting out magazine pictures that speak to a theme you're exploring or including images that represent feelings that are present for you is another way to include visuals in your journal. Draw with colored pencils in the margins or all over the page. Add stickers, glitter, dried leaves, or flowers. Judy, one of the participants in my writing groups, creates doodles inside

borders on some of her journal pages. Let your creativity come forth in any ways that you choose.

6. Use "bridging activities," for example, meditation, stretching, simple breathing exercises, listening to music, taking a short walk, or any other centering process before you write in your journal. Bridging activities can help you transition from other activities or frames of mind to the reflective process of journaling. Even three to five minutes of an activity that will help you relax and connect with yourself can put you in a "journal friendly" frame of mind, ready to drop into a period of rich connection with yourself. Sometimes I take five minutes to do "What's So Writing" as a way to give voice to whatever's going on with me in the present moment. One of my clients, Eileen, who is a high school teacher, introduced "present-centered" writing to her students as a way to start the school day. She had them write whatever "was so" for them in their notebooks for ten to fifteen minutes. She noticed that whenever they did this, they were more attentive and engaged for the first morning activity. The students dubbed this exercise "What's So Writing." I may write about feeling tired, exhilarated or, perhaps, I'm still carrying on an earlier conversation with my daughter in my mind that needs to be expressed on paper for it to be released. It's a technique that can shift you from head to heart, body, or feelings.

7. If your commitment to journaling starts to feel like a burdensome task and you notice yourself becoming resistant to this writing, check in with yourself to see if journaling has become a should rather than a want. It's important to remember that this is not a school

homework assignment and that no external authority is looking over your shoulder demanding that you do this. For those of us who grew up in families or attended schools where strict rules were imposed on us and we were reprimanded, sometimes harshly, if we didn't toe the line, almost any project or activity that we want to commit to can easily and quickly start to seem obligatory. Then our "inner teenagers" rebel against what feels like rigid rules, and we may end up turning our backs on something that we actually love to do. I see people do this regularly with meditation and all kinds of creative projects. What originally started out as "I want to...." has now become "I should...." You may also feel guilty because you are not following through on a commitment you made to yourself. This is a painful state to be in and often accompanies the "should syndrome."

An effective strategy for counteracting what Psychologist Fritz Perls called "the tyranny of the shoulds" is to write a list of why you want to journal, including how it benefits you, makes you feel when you do it, etc. You can keep this list as a reminder in a place where you can easily see it, or make a new list when you experience resistance to journaling because it has become a should. Remembering why you *want* to journal can re-ignite your passion.

EXERCISES AND ACTIVITIES

Journaling Techniques

1. Stream Writing. As discussed earlier, stream writing—sometimes called free writing, deep writing, or free association writing—is a journaling device

in which you simply start writing, do not censor what is coming forth, and keep writing until you feel complete. You let go of control and become willing to not know where you're going. You can do stream writing in response to a general theme, for example, boundaries, or a specific theme, like a communication difficulty you're having with a family member, or you can do open-ended stream writing. With the latter, you simply start from wherever you are in the present moment and let words spill out, expressing feelings, thoughts, or physical sensations. This is the same as "What's So Writing," only you're doing it for a longer period and not simply doing it as a way to make a transition to something else. If you write more than just thoughts and ideas, you are likely to access your unconscious and may be surprised at what you discover. Feelings or images may rise to the surface, as may insights and profound realizations. People experience many aha! moments as a result of stream writing.

2. Lists. Lists are a way to succinctly capture and express ideas, feelings, insights, observations, beliefs, and anything else that you want to focus on and explore. I love lists! They are a short method of capturing essentials in any area of your life. With regard to your caregiving, for example, on any given day you can list what you liked about your experiences that day and what you disliked, what you learned, what made you happy, what saddened or frustrated you, and perhaps, what resources you could draw upon or what you might do to make the next day a bit easier. The list of what you can list is endless!

You can also use one or more items on any list as a prompt for a longer piece of writing. For example, if you list activities that you love to do, such as hike, listen to classical music, or play with your cat, you can choose any one or more of these and write a lot about them. You may write about what you enjoy about hiking, what you don't like about hiking, where the best trails are, or your best and worst experiences.

3. Inquiry and review. This is a process that consists of posing questions to yourself in your journal with regard to a specific area of growth you want to focus on or a quality you want to develop or strengthen. You can do this once a day or two to three times a week if that is preferable. You respond to the same questions each time you write, tracking and reviewing how you're progressing in this area. Some possible questions related to well-being that you can include in your journal are: When was I centered today? What did being centered feel like—mentally, physically, emotionally, and spiritually? When was I off? What did that feel like? Who were my teachers today? What did I learn? What obstacles did I encounter? How did I deal with them? What is a good way to begin tomorrow? Let's say that you want to experience more equanimity. You're reactive more than you want to be. You want to feel calmer and experience more evenness. You could ask yourself questions, such as when did I experience equanimity today? What did equanimity feel like—mentally, physically, emotionally, and spiritually? When did I experience it the least? What did that feel like? What kept me from experiencing equanimity today? What obstacles did I encounter?

How did I deal with them? What did I learn? What's a good way to begin tomorrow?

4. Unsent letters. Unsent letters are a powerful writing tool for giving voice to what you are reluctant or afraid to say to another person or, perhaps, what you just never had the opportunity to share because they are no longer in your life. Like stream writing, this is an opportunity to do uncensored writing, giving voice to thoughts and feelings within you that want to be expressed. You may need to write numerous letters to someone about one or more experiences that you haven't been able to speak about. This letter provides a means for you to release pent up feelings or share secrets, memories, hopes, or dreams. You may want to express grief or anger in this writing, or what you deeply want to share may be love or gratitude. Unsent letters can be written for people who are currently in your life, people whom you may not have seen for a long time, or people that have died. I wrote numerous letters to my brother after he died in 1982, and it was profoundly cathartic for me. Feelings came out in this writing that I had not been able to access in any other way.

    I wrote an unsent letter to Heidi a couple of years after her diagnosis. I needed to put into words how difficult it had been for me to see the pain she had to endure throughout those years. I cried a lot as the pain from my hurting heart cascaded onto the pages of my journal. Staying with this, I remembered times when she was a toddler that I wasn't emotionally available to her because I was wrapped up in my own personal difficulties. I sobbed some more and expressed deep regret in the letter. I apologized and told her that I was making it up to her now and would continue to be there for her always. This single letter was transformative. Not only did I touch into feelings that had been suppressed for years, but I also realized that I needed to talk to Heidi more about her early childhood and my lack of full presence then. I knew I needed to apologize, to make amends. That amends-making conversation marked a turning point in our relationship. She was so thankful that I told her these truths, and I felt as if I had released a burden that I was unknowingly carrying for many years. We held each other, and both cried for a long time.

5. Inner Dialogues. As I mentioned in the "Meet Your Creative Selves" exercise in Chapter Four—Creativity is Good Medicine, our personalities are comprised of many different parts called subpersonalities. You can get a sense of this by reflecting on the different aspects of yourself that come out at different times; for example, you may express the assertive, confident part of yourself in professional settings and the playful, spontaneous part when you are with friends playing charades. The frightened or hurt child may move to the foreground when someone judges or rejects you. When we dialogue with these parts, we discover how they came to be the way they are, and we let them express thoughts and feelings that may have been hidden from us for years. Learning to listen to these different aspects of ourselves and getting to the deeper layers of wounding that are often at their core is a powerful way to develop self acceptance and move toward wholeness.

Here is an example of a subpersonality dialogue with your inner child:

> You: I'd like to connect with you, little Ronnie. Will you talk to me?
>
> Ronnie: I feel pretty upset right now.
>
> You: Why are you upset?
>
> Ronnie: My feelings got hurt, and I was so scared when Jarrett was yelling at you. I'm still scared, and I feel like hiding in a corner where no one can find me.
>
> You: How can I help you?
>
> Ronnie: I'd like you to listen to me when I'm scared instead of pretending I don't exist.
>
> You: Do you feel like I'm listening to you now and that you can talk?
>
> Ronnie: Kinda. I have more to say, though.

You can dialogue in your journal with the wounded parts of yourself and with your strengths, gifts, and talents. For example, you probably have an effective communicator within you, a compassionate part, and a responsible subpersonality, as well. Dialoguing with your strengths, as well as your wounded parts, is a way to further strengthen your positive qualities, develop potentials, and discover what these subpersonalities need to grow and become stronger and well-integrated into your life.

6. Sentence Completion. Completing sentence stems is a journaling technique that can help you get to the essence of a feeling, situation, or issue. Here

is another writing tool in which you bypass your reasoning mind and dip into the unconscious by giving yourself permission to write without analysis or conscious thought.

You can create the beginning of a sentence about anything at all. For example, I'm afraid of.... I wish that.... What I need to do for myself is.... What I'm learning in this situation is.... Keep completing the sentence without censoring or stopping to think about what to write. Keep your hand moving on the page. If nothing comes to you, just draw squiggly lines until words naturally come forth. Take five minutes for each sentence stem, and work with as few or as many as you would like.

Sentence stems can build on each other, as well. If you write, I wish I had more energy, the next sentence stem might be: To have more energy, I can.... You'll be surprised at the insights that will come to you from using this simple technique.

Chapter 7

CAREGIVERS SPEAK: STORIES AND WISDOM FROM CAREGIVERS

We learn best by experience. We learn next best by hearing of others' shared experiences. I interviewed four family and four professional caregivers, asking them questions about self-care, the rewards and challenges of caregiving, boundaries, and other topics that I've explored in this book, *Soul Care for Caregivers*. I also asked each person what advice they have for other caregivers. Here are their stories and the wisdom they have to share with you.

*

Leah is forty-eight years old, a graphic artist, and mother of two children—Eric, age ten, and Sarah, age fifteen. When Eric was seven, he started exhibiting behaviors that worried Leah and her husband, Frank. Initially, Eric had to touch things twice to feel safe. Then, he had to touch things five, ten, and then more than twenty times. He also repeatedly turned light switches on and off and had to do that the same number of times each time. Eventually, he was diagnosed with Obsessive Compulsive Disorder. "It was a terrifying period," Leah said. "We had so much trouble finding the right specialist and the care that suited him. It was a very long process, and his mental and emotional suffering just kept escalating. The hardest thing for me has been to see him suffer and not be able to help him. I think this is every mother's worst fear. I'd call the therapist in tears, pleading with her to tell me what to do. "I don't know how to help him," I'd say. Being unable to make it better for him was devastating. It's horrifying to see your child acting in a way that is abnormal. He's on medication now, so he's improved, but we still deal with OCD on a daily basis."

In the first year, another difficulty Leah faced was the fact that the entire focus of the family became OCD. Frank and Leah tried to normalize things as much as they could so that this didn't take over their lives, especially since they had another child. "Sarah is five years older and is a very understanding girl, but she definitely felt both neglected and left out at times. His behavior scared her, too. She saw some OCD tendencies in herself, which really unnerved her. She went through a period where everything had to be even. Once she scraped her knee, then she had to intentionally scrape the other one so they were even," Leah recalled.

"It's particularly hard when the person you're caring for is so young," said Leah. "Eric's always been very shy and wouldn't talk much to people so I had to do a lot of talking for him. If someone asked him a question, he'd whisper the answer to me and I would speak for him. It was also frightening to hold our ground at times when we didn't feel like it was good for him to act out some of his behaviors. It was very upsetting to him if we intervened. It was also difficult for me to say "no" to things that would give him some pleasure, like watching extra TV or staying up late. What I did was to learn as much about the disorder as I could so that I could help him learn to fight it. I became the one the rest of the family looked to regarding how to deal with a situation when it would arise. I took it upon myself to fight the battle for him since he was too young to do it. I was scared and overwhelmed, but it helped me to feel like I was making a difference."

Sharing their experiences with others is a challenge for some caregivers, and one that Leah came up against. She knew that it would help her if she were to process her feelings with people she knew, but she was reluctant to do that. "Mental illness still has a stigma," she said. "If I were to open up as fully as I needed to, I wanted to be sure that whoever I was talking to could really hold all this. Also, I was concerned about Eric's privacy. Would he want lots of people to know about his struggles? I have one friend who has a background in psychology, and I've talked to her a lot over these last three years. She's been a saving grace. But I can't turn to her every day, so there's a buildup of my own emotional reactions to the whole situation. Who else besides Barbara would I talk to? How often? When?"

Initially, as is true for many of us, Leah took very little time to care for her own needs. "Self-care wasn't high on my priority list. It always seemed so much more important to take care of Eric and the rest of the family. And a lot of my time was taken up by keeping "life things" from slipping through the cracks." She did find that learning about the illness reduced her stress because it made her feel that there was something she could do. "When we finally found the right specialist and his symptoms began to abate, I did focus at least a bit on taking care of myself. Walking in nature helped me discharge some of that energy. Journal writing is another helpful tool. It's great to have a safe place to pour out everything inside. I didn't have to keep it inside anymore."

Leah advises caregivers to reach out to others whom you can talk to openly or who are going through something similar. This is why many caregivers seek out and join support groups. "Don't hesitate to get help sooner than later. Psychological issues get more ingrained and harder to fight if you don't deal with them early on." She also urges caregivers not to feel guilty about letting self-care be a priority. "The more you fill yourself up, the more you have to give," she said. She also said that it was very hard to trust anything when things were going so badly, but she advises family caregivers to find little windows of trust and focus in on them. "Fan that flame, even a little bit," Leah recommends. "It can hold you in times when you can't reach it." Many of us discover our strengths as a result of caregiving, as Leah did. "It's been a gift to have been able to hang in there with Eric. At times, it felt like everything was crumbling, and I was the remaining pillar. It made me see my own capabilities." She also indicated that these experiences made her relationship with Eric much better. "He can talk to me more about things the average ten-year-old never talks to his mother about. We've gotten very close as a result of this."

*

Thom, age sixty-one, is a personal and professional coach. His son, Adam, now twenty, started having up to two hundred seizures a day when he was one year old and was later diagnosed with four-quadrant seizure disorder. Thom has been a single parent for eighteen years and the primary caregiver for his son.

"I put all of myself into caring for Adam and finding the right treatments," he said. "I was also learning everything I could about the condition and researching every alternative and traditional treatment I could find. He had a lot of problems when he started school. I was at his school constantly dealing with those issues. Caregiving was a fulltime job, and I had to work as well. For me, the greatest challenge was that I wasn't mommy. Not being able to be a mommy for my son was unbearable at times. I was also angry with his mother for not being more involved. His health and well-being contributed to the difficulties in our marriage and to our eventual separation."

Caregiving for Adam was very difficult emotionally in many ways. The full impact of this dimension of caregiving is often misunderstood or minimized. "Our feelings got mixed together. I merged with him. I was overinvolved, putting my nose into his business more than I should have, intruding upon his privacy. I was overprotective and fearful. I felt responsible for making him okay and guilty when I couldn't. It's still very hard for me to step back and not give. I'm in giving mode all the time. I used to feel like I was putting pressure on him to be well."

Thom didn't express his fear, frustration, and anger directly to Adam because he didn't want to burden him. These feelings, though, came out in the form of overreactions. "I'd express much stronger feelings than particular events warranted," said Thom. "I didn't feel like I had a right to my feelings. In retrospect, I see that I was constantly in fear. I never knew when he was going to have a seizure or when he might fall. He got bullied in school, so I was constantly worried about that. I drank too much at the time and knew I was doing it to numb out."

Thom had very little support for most of those years. "I had some friends," he said, "but I always felt guilty asking for help because most folks were scared about the seizures, especially if they needed to be alone with him. My friendships were affected. I was no longer available; I lost people and stopped participating in activities I'd been involved in. My relationship with my daughter, Abby, who was three years older than Adam, was strained, as well, because the whole house was about Adam," Thom noted. "My self-care was inadequate. I did work out at the gym, and that was a place I got my feelings out. We lived near the woods, and I spent as much time as I could walking there. I had sleep problems and was exhausted a lot of the time."

As difficult as taking care of Adam was, Thom found caregiving to be transformational. "Adam is my greatest teacher. I didn't understand what compassion or listening were. I had to be fully present and never knew how to be present before. It made me an excellent life coach and teacher. The sensitivity and empathy that I have today are due to Adam. I've learned how to be someone's champion, not just their nurse. He taught me how to connect with people where they are, not where I am. The majority of skills I have today in relating to others, I learned from being a caregiver. I learned how to be in an intimate relationship." Thom clearly exemplifies the many rewards that can come from caregiving.

Thom advises family caregivers to respect their care receiver in every way and to see them for who they are, not who we want them to be. "This is very hard when you want them to be whole and healthy," says Thom. "Showing love is fifty percent nurturing and fifty percent respect." He also learned that the only way to be really effective is to take care of yourself. "When I started taking care of myself, I was three times the caregiver that I was before." His self-care practices now include a healthy diet, working out, meditation, prayer, and emotional processing. "I want to make sure I don't bring my issues to my son. I also ask more of Adam now. I ask him to help me and to make a contribution in the household. This was hard to do initially, but it's been good for both of us."

*

Rowena, age sixty-seven, retired, is the primary care-giver for her eighty-eight-year-old mother, Irene, who has a heart condition and has been in assisted living for over four years. Rowena receives some help from her grand-daughter, but it is sporadic.

Caregiving often catalyzes unresolved family issues, such as mother/daughter dynamics, which represented the greatest challenge for Rowena. "If things aren't done "just so," Mom can get cool; she withdraws. Then I back away, too, in response to her. It's easier to keep my heart open when she is more open. When she shuts down, I shut down. I react to her moods and emotional states a lot more than I want to. I'm handling all the practical and financial matters and trying to be some kind of emo-tional support for her at the same time. I do all kinds of things without telling her because all the financial and legal issues that come up would be too much for her. I also don't tell her because I want to avoid the inevitable criticisms about the way I'm managing things. When I was growing up, and for most of my life, I felt like I could never meet up to her expectations for the way that things should be done. That whole issue has gotten even more intense since I've become her caregiver.

I often feel unacknowledged, underappreciated, and overwhelmed. I'm not seen for how much I do." Many caregivers are not fully acknowledged for all the contribu-tions they make. They commonly feel undervalued and, often, invisible.

Rowena feels that self-care is an absolute necessity. "I'm getting a lot better with it," she says. "I'm finding the exact formula for balance now. When I get overwhelmed, I see it's because I'm falling behind in my self-care. I don't get depleted when I tend to my needs. Self-care is the dial I'm honing in on. Nature is a healing balm for me. My main tool is writing. I also make collages, greeting cards, and fool around with some crafts. I practically jump up and down with glee with these things. I'm so happy I'm following through with this. I feel good just going into the crafts store and buying things without knowing what I'll do with them. Whenever I can, I take a half-day of silence. I designed a home retreat. I need solitude. I need to do it on a more regular basis."

Rowena said that she was shocked by the intense, harsh emotions that came up in her in the early months of her caregiving. "Feelings came up that I've never allowed or felt before. I had this picture of being calm and steady if I had to take care of my mother, but that's not how things have turned out at all. As hard as this has been emotionally, I've discovered that I'm stronger than I thought I was. This experience has taken me to profound emotional and spiritual depths that I hadn't expected.

I've learned to focus on the now, to keep my attention off both the past and the future. This has given me an opportunity to learn what keeps me from loving and being open. Someone told me a while ago that my mother is my teacher. I pushed that aside then, but now I see that it's true. I get to see how attached I am to these old patterns of reaction. Lately, I'm noticing that I do have more compassion towards myself, less self-criticism. I'm not as much of a perfectionist now as I was earlier. I can see that I'm doing the best I can in a very difficult situation. When I'm really up against it, I write Soul Letters and ask for guidance about how to handle whatever stuck place I'm in. I get extremely helpful advice," she said.

When I asked Rowena about boundaries and limit-setting, she remarked that it's still frightening for her to set limits but she sets them anyway. "I center myself before I get involved in something with her. I carefully plan my time when to phone and when to go to see her. She often balks at my plans or any limitations I establish, trying to take over and change things to suit her. I'm embarrassed to say that I do often yield to her. We went out on Easter, and she said "no" to the time and the restaurant, after telling me to name a time and select a restaurant. It threw me into a tizzy, and I just capitulated. These are the hardest moments for me. It feels like she won and I lost. I regress. These situations are getting further and further apart, though."

The value and importance of self-care was at the top of the list for Rowena's advice to other family caregivers. "Learning to stay present and non-reactive is imperative, too," she said, "as is learning to listen, really listen. If I'm present when I'm listening to Mom, I care better for her. I'm not distracted. I'm more open. Getting support is important, too. I looked for caregiver support for the first few years and couldn't find it. The isolation is very hard."

*

James, age fifty-one, is the primary caregiver for his significant other, Emily. Emily, age fifty-four, has kidney disease and is in the process of preparing for a kidney transplant.

"Her condition became very serious about a year ago," he said. "Emily has only wanted to do alternative therapies for years, and as much as I'm also drawn to alternatives to Western medicine, I felt differently when things got so critical. She had to be hospitalized, which was highly stressful for her, and I experienced more stress going through that with her than I had in ten years. My hands were tied; I was very worried. Just having to convince her that she had to go to the hospital was very difficult. She assumes I'll respect her views. Her parents expect that I'll modulate her views. I get caught in the middle, but the worst of all of it is my worry about her. My own employment situation is stressful, as well. I can't take on engineering contracts because my attention and time is required for the care of Emily, and I'm also the kidney donor for her."

The amount and range of stressors that family caregivers experience often astounds me. I admire them so much for their courage, strength, and commitment to their loved ones. The word courage comes from the French word *coeur*, meaning heart.

James said that the greatest gift for him has been the deepened intimacy with Emily. "The other person is so vulnerable," he said. "This involves a whole other level of being there for someone. It builds trust."

With regard to boundaries, James said that what was most challenging for him was to have to monitor Emily's diet, supplements, and medications. "I hate nagging," he said. "And she's more forgetful than I am. I'm more of a creature of habit. Diet is very important in her condition. It's difficult to be as strict as you need to be, and I constantly check on her. Also, you can't ever skip the antirejection drug, which is coming up after the transplant. My way of doing things is the way she's going to have to do things. I don't feel good about having to impose my ways of being on others. I like people to just live the way they choose to live. This makes me feel controlling; it stretches me way beyond my comfort zone."

I asked James how he deals with stressors. He said that the anxiety goes away when he takes his attention off of it. "I'm not anxious about donating my kidney or having all the tests. I do have anxiety that all these health tests might find a health problem that I haven't known about. I also worry about our two families meeting, which will happen for the first time. They're as different as you could imagine—politically, socioeconomically—everything. Emily and I won't be there for each other when we come out of anesthesia. We'll be surrounded by family."

"Walking up on the mountain that's near our house and being in nature is very healing for me. I want to find a way to meditate more. It's great to move into a state where anxiety and emotional turmoil drop away for a time. I do tend to take on others' emotional energies and haven't been managing this very well lately. Taking time alone, walking, and meditating releases it. I'm getting better and better with self-care."

James' advice for other caregivers is to "allow for the mystery." He said that you don't know how events will unfold. "Learn to trust in life and yourself, that you'll deal with whatever comes up as it unfolds."

*

Alice, age seventy, is recently retired after over forty-five years of medical and surgical nursing. "My greatest challenge," she said, "was simply having too much to do and not enough time to do it. Too many patients needed our attention at the same time. Before the four-to-one nurse to patient ratio in California, we had much bigger assignments. It was overwhelming at times, and many of us were highly stressed. Every time I'd go off the ward, I was asking myself if I got it all done, if I did everything I was supposed to do. Did my patients receive adequate care? Would anyone get hurt? That stress was always there in the background."

Alice recalled her career beginnings. "In the early years of my nursing career, there was no recognition or attention given to our emotional states. You needed to just deal with your own emotional reactions, and that takes time, training, and support. There's still not very much of that available. I experienced too much suffering, and that didn't shift for me until I became secure and well-established in my own life."

Alice said that it had always been rich and rewarding to serve and that she always had a feeling of service as a nurse. "Contributing what I could to the patients' comfort and well-being made me feel good about myself. I never had the feeling I wasn't doing something worthwhile with my life. I like nurses. They're good people. Most are "people people" and are generous. They care for you and about you. I did have to choose over and over again to be in the face of suffering. It was a clear and conscious choice I had to make repeatedly."

Alice said that it is a gift and privilege to be there for people at their death. "It is a miracle," she said, "to witness how many people become peaceful about dying. To be able to provide the environment where peacefulness can happen was deeply rewarding. Compassion grew in me."

With regard to boundaries, Alice learned early on that taking cases home with her didn't work. "I learned not to worry and not to take it home unless there's something to be done. You won't survive over the long run if you don't learn how to leave your patients at the hospital when your shift is over. This is something that many helping professionals learn about the hard way. They report feeling exhausted and overwhelmed because it seems like their patients are with them twenty-four hours a day. They are constantly thinking about them, often not knowing how to turn off their minds." Alice is one of the fortunate ones who has learned how to detach.

"It wasn't until the mid-eighties that I discovered the importance of self-care," Alice said. "I did some personal transformational work that helped to shine a light on this. Before that, I exercised intermittently, complained a lot, and went to lots of movies. I always had many friends and an active social life, which helped a lot with stress. As a result of the personal growth work, I started to meditate, exercise regularly, and keep a journal. The journal is still a healing practice for me."

The advice that Alice offers to other caregivers is to make a priority of self-care. "It is absolutely essential," she said. She also recommends that caregivers acknowledge the self-destructive nature of fear and worry. "Find the value of letting go of worry. Also, have some kind of social network. When my father was dying, I decided that I'd never do anything this hard alone."

*

Darren, age thirty-six, is a psychotherapist who's been in private practice for seven years. He works with men and women, couples, and groups. For one-and-a-half years, he worked in a group home with severely emotionally disturbed children, aged six to twelve.

In discussing the challenges of being a psychotherapist, Darren said that he'd had the most difficult time with self-care, a theme so commonly echoed by caregivers. "I can still feel drained and depleted from being in difficult places with people," he said. "Their most challenging material and defenses against that often surface in sessions. I can get pulled into places in their psychic world, which doesn't serve either of us. Also, people have directed their aggressive, desperate energies at me, and this can activate my fear response and nervous system to a great degree. In the group home, the children had a hard time containing themselves if I didn't come in completely prepared with a full plan. I learned to be very present, structured, and clear."

Darren continues to discover many rewards from his work. "People are starving to be deeply seen and understood for who they are. Finding someone who provides that for them is like finding water in the desert. I love providing this deep nourishment to people by seeing their authentic self. Also, I get to see the humanity and full range of human behavior. I've come to see what is similar about us. There are jewels inside of everyone, no matter what their behaviors and actions. I've worked with people who are pretty dishonest in the world and cruel in relationships."

Darren says that he has a lot of respect for people who come in and do this deep psychological work because it's not easy. "There's a willingness to say I can't do it on my own," he said. "There's so much focus on self-sufficiency in this culture. So many people that I've seen are willing to examine their behavior, willing to see the part they played in their broken relationships, for example. That really inspires me. This work has softened me," said Darren. "It has taken me out of a mindset where someone is better than someone else. It has helped me accept people for who they are and see that we're all doing the best we can.

Self-care is one of the most important issues to address: the number of clients I see each day, space between sessions, always checking in with myself to see what will nourish me. I only spend time with friends who nourish me, not those who drain me. When I started working in the group home, I found myself letting go of all kinds of unhealthy relationships. I cook. The more I buy and cook food, the better I feel. I need alone time and am protective of my time and energy. It helps me to have people to check in with when I'm stuck. That helps guide me back toward myself if I'm feeling disconnected." Darren has been able to take what he's learned personally about self-care back into his work with clients. "I ask my clients to become clear about the impact of others on them—who is nourishing, who isn't. A lot of work I do with clients is about their own self-care and helping them discover what is nurturing for them."

Darren advises caregivers not to lose themselves in the role of caregiver. "Our attention can become overly attuned to others," he said. He believes that caregivers need to learn how to attune to themselves outside of their role. "We are not the change agents," said Darren. "I try not to take responsibility for what happens in the room. Some therapists see themselves as the one who is healing, the one who is responsible for the transformation that is taking place. A better way to think about that is: I'm present. I'm curious and interested in what's happening, what wants to be expressed. There's an organic process of growth that happens, and my role is to trust the process and trust that my clients want to be whole. I point them back to themselves. I'm not the force of change. I'm supporting a process that I think wants to happen, that has a lot more wisdom than I do."

He also feels that caregivers shouldn't be attached to outcomes, to clients getting to a certain point that you think they could get to. "Don't take either their successes or failures personally," he said. "Try not to believe their projections that you're the greatest person in the world. Just take it all in as part of the process. On other days, you may be the worst person in the world. Don't take that in either."

*

Christina, age forty-one, is an educator and somatic practitioner. She specializes in working with people who experience post-traumatic stress, including the homeless and survivors of natural disasters, such as the tsunami survivors in India.

Christina acknowledged many rewards of caregiving. She indicated that she has grown in her capacity to face what's inside of her and to be a steady presence for others.

"Also," she said, "my faith in the goodness of life has grown by seeing the courage and coherence of the human spirit and body. I love the trust, vulnerability, and sacredness of accompanying someone on the journey of healing. I have been given a special window into the depths of human suffering and how we share that burden—how alone and how together we are in that struggle.

The more I remain grounded and connected to myself, the more it supports my clients in being able to contain their own experience. When I'm grounded, I'm aware of the thoughts, feelings, and sensations in my body. Being present to myself in this way creates an open space for me to receive the client. I teach the people I work with how to witness and comfort themselves in their experience without being overwhelmed by it. Being centered and grounded helps so much in alleviating the stressors of caregiving. We're able to access our inner resources, and we become less depleted. This helps us to maintain healthy boundaries, as well."

She related that it isn't always easy to remain centered and resilient. "If I become too identified or feel too emotionally impacted by what someone has gone through, I can become dislocated from myself, and then I don't do my best work. My ongoing goal is to stay connected to my bigger spiritual identity. What's most challenging, and also most rewarding, is when the person I'm working with has no sense of hope or possibility and I'm able to help them access a deeper level of support within themselves. A part of me has known those dark places, and I draw upon my own spiritual resources to help my clients through those dark places."

When Christina was in India, she worked in a makeshift clinic where she could see people for only one session. "They have been through this horrific life event," she said, "and I have to keep letting go of my attachment to the outcome and what will come next. I invest myself fully, then let go and see that I'm part of a larger system of help, that there are other resources for this person to draw on, including their existing community. Whether I see my clients only once or on a regular basis, I always give them practices to work with at home to help build their resilience."

Christina believes that tending to mind, body, and spirit is of paramount importance. "I practice yoga every day. I take time to be alone. It's important for me to rest, eat, exercise, and sleep in ways that keep me balanced. I also need to partake of spiritual nourishment, whether it's in formal or random moments of meditation, and to expose myself to great wisdom through teachers, books, audios, or videos. I love to take in the energy of people of great realization; they inspire me to keep evolving. If I don't tend to self-care, I can get frazzled and tend to over-promise and under-deliver. If I didn't take such good care of myself, I couldn't give as much as I do, and I could become physically ill and psychologically imbalanced—depressed, anxious, confused. Then, I would not be a good resource for my clients."

She recommends that caregivers incorporate somatic practices in their work, as these techniques help clients slow down, nourish themselves, and come into present time. "For example, I tell my clients to bring attention to the physical sensations in their legs and feet, and I do so myself. This area tends to be a neutral, grounding place to focus and doing so actually helps drain excessive energy from emotions and thoughts. Whenever I tell a client to do so, I follow suit, and I use this technique between and after sessions to discharge energy." Christina believes that body-centered methods can help caregivers avoid burnout and recover more quickly when they are out of balance.

She also feels that it's important to stay connected to what inspires you. "Everyone has personal resources they love to draw upon for renewal and strength. For some, it's being out in nature; for others, it might be cuddling a beloved animal or engaging in a creative activity, such as dance, music, or art."

"Everyone is a giver and receiver of care," she said. "It seems important to normalize the whole field of care so that there's less stigma around receiving support and less grandiosity about giving support. Giving and receiving care are such natural and necessary parts of our lives."

*

Johanna, age forty-three, is a mental health specialist who works in the classroom in inner city schools, with children and teens, ages three to nineteen. She specializes in violence prevention in children.

Johanna said that her greatest challenge was gaining access to teachers and students. She was given physical access, but she needed personal access in order to be fully engaged and so that her presence was accepted. She said that teachers could be resistant to her because they felt watched and that the students with the most trauma felt watched, as well. "Once they understand that I'm there to assist them, they open up to me. It takes time, though. Also, dealing with the level of trauma in the children that I see every day is unsettling. I have to stay away from thinking that I can't treat these kids, that I can't help them because they're so deeply traumatized. It is so unsettling to ponder that there are parents who are completely unavailable to their children mentally and physically, who harm them and expose them to harm, who don't provide safety, and who have no understanding of the effects of parental care on their children. Most of these children are so emotionally incapacitated that they are unable to form positive attachments. They can't avail themselves of what is offered to them. I have, though, been able to gain their trust, which is very gratifying. It's been very hard work because they need so much emotional support. Also, I've had to learn to pull back and not take their negativity and attacks personally."

Johanna deals with stress by staying in contact with and getting support from colleagues who are experienced in the field. In addition, she joined a gym when she began this work because she knew that working out would help relieve tension and stress. "I've maintained my gym membership," said Johanna. "It's one of the best things I do for myself.

The rewards of this work are enormous. When a teacher eventually welcomes me, it feels wonderful. I've developed rich connections with many of them. The rewards from working with these children are extraordinary. They develop trust. They have been able to experience and verbalize positive emotions. Many of them have reached out to me, wanting to help with projects at the school. They're also so happy to see me, which is very gratifying.

I've become more humble and aware since I've been doing this work. I've learned that there's so much more to people than what's on the surface and I no longer form immediate judgments about people or situations. I slow down when I can, step back, and reflect when a situation presents itself. 'Let's take a look at this,' I think. You have to be very present, in the moment, and sometimes, you have to be quick and act on your feet. I've learned to rely on my intuition in those moments. More than ever now, I look for the positive in people and learn from who they are and what they have to say."

Regarding boundaries, Johanna said that she's had to separate her work life from her home life. "I have an eighteen-year-old," she said. "When I'm home, I'm fully home. I had to learn not to be consumed by my work. It was easy to come home and do "just one more report." Stopping this was very hard to do. Also, when working in an environment where emotional needs are severe, it's difficult to turn that off when you leave work. It's tempting to keep thinking about and looking for the best solutions and resources and wondering about what I may have missed that day. Without good boundaries, you become emotionally and physically depleted. I've also found that the families and friends of the children want to communicate with me about their personal problems. I've had to set limits about this, too." Here again, we see how maintaining healthy boundaries can greatly enhance our caregiving and is an essential ingredient in self-care.

In offering advice to other caregivers, Johanna said that if you don't take care of yourself, you have nothing to offer. "You can't be present with others," she said. "'Physician, know thyself.' We need to know and be attuned to our own needs. This is often lacking in the helping professions." Johanna also recommended that professional caregivers do volunteer work in their communities. "Volunteer work helps me stay humble, and it develops my empathy. It also helps me to stay connected to others outside of my work and to feel a part of my community. The rewards of giving where you're not getting are enormous. It increases your capacity to experience life and fills you as a person."

Chapter 8

PRACTICING WHAT I TEACH

I received another one of those "phone calls," you know, the ones we dread, the ones that surprise us very late at night or, worse, in the middle of the night or way too early in the morning. Or the call could come at a decent hour, but the voice on the other end is hushed, deadly serious, crying, even sobbing, broken, or frantic.

This most recent call from Mom triggered painful phone memories. 1982. The police: "Do you know Scott Friedman?

"Yes. I'm his sister," I said, gripping the edge of the kitchen counter to brace myself.

"We found his driver's license in a backpack in a car that he'd abandoned. Your name and phone number were in it. I'm sorry to tell you this, but he jumped off of the Golden Gate Bridge. He was unconscious when we got to him, and he died about an hour later."

I remember very little after that, except some words about needing to go to the morgue to identify his body. Memories of other alarming calls flash through my mind—the hospital when Dad was dying telling me that I should come back because "it was time," Heidi's call in 1989 announcing the diagnosis of a "bad disease," and her call a couple of years ago after she got the results of the amniocentesis letting her know that her baby had Down syndrome.

Mom hadn't sounded like this since Dad died in 1992. "Susie, I need to go to the emergency room. Right away. Dr. Levin told me to go. Can you and John take me?"

"What's wrong?" I ask. I'm on red alert and start to panic, matching the panic in my mother's voice.

"Terrible stomach pain. Really terrible." Her voice is weak and cracking.

My thoughts start racing. How bad is this? Serious? Must be, if he's sending her to the emergency room. Is she overreacting? Why is she so scared? Never had terrible stomach pain that I knew about. Try to relax. Deep breaths. Be steady.

"We'll leave right now, Mom. If this gets unbearable, call 911."

In the car, I remember Heidi having to take me to the emergency room with what turned out to be second and third degree burns on my abdomen from having accidentally spilled a pot of boiling water on myself. She was only half there until she heard the doctor's pronouncement about the severity of the burns. I knew she had been thinking what I'm thinking now—drama. Mom overreacting again. Turns out I wasn't, and maybe my mother isn't either. I think, "I don't know. Just be calm and kind to her. I hope we get there soon."

We arrive. Five p.m. and she still has her robe on. Pale. Trembling. I feel badly for her and worried about what this is all about. Thank goodness for John and his calm, steady presence. I feel immensely grateful that he is who he is and that he always has my back. I know that he's aware that this is way outside of my comfort zone. He'll be with me every step of the way, I think to myself. Anytime John senses I need support, he's there in the healthiest of ways, not smothering or intrusive, or doing what he knows I can do for myself. So here he is, effortlessly, or so it seems, tending to both of us. I am reminded of how fortunate I am and how long it took to find Mr. Right.

We're at the emergency room for about eight hours, and Mom is diagnosed with diverticulitis and a urinary infection. They also found some "old" kidney stones and weren't clear at that point how problematic that could be. She is released with medication and a dietary regimen and told to call her doctor the next day.

This was the beginning of an eight-month journey into waxing and waning symptoms, insomnia, fatigue, weight loss, and depression. For me, it was an eight-month journey back into the challenges and rewards of caregiving—everything that this book is about. I had been given another opportunity to practice what I teach. "Read my book to me," I jokingly said to John. "I need it."

I thought of the irony and the perfection of having an intense caregiving experience right in the middle of writing this book. There hadn't been any long or serious relapses with Heidi for at least two years, so I had a reprieve from the very difficult emotional and physical aspects of family caregiving. Being in those trenches again, I was more gratified than ever that I had written this book. Reminded of how stressful family caregiving is, I was also aware of the possibilities for growth and transformation that stressful events like this present to us. I also rediscovered how essential it is to make self-care a priority and to find every possible inner and outer resource that's available. My empathy for other caregivers increased exponentially, as did my motivation to bring whatever I can to the world of caregiver education and support.

Many of you who are family caregivers are now, have been, or could one day be in similar circumstances. From one minute to the next, your world is turned upside down. The phone rings, or you open an email, and your life changes. The change that has been catalyzed may have put you on a course that will last days, weeks, months, or even years. For some of you, there won't be a return to your life as it was before this event. Some of you may have been mentally prepared for this; others haven't even considered that their life could take a turn in this direction. For those who've known this was likely to occur, the day-to-day realities and challenges of caregiving often come as a big surprise. In fact, there are surprises all along the path of caregiving.

During this time, Heidi had a flare up of Crohn's. The worrying parts of my brain were getting a great workout. I felt the crunch of being in the sandwich generation, as many baby-boomers are: caring for children and grand-children, and aging parents. Heidi, very fortunately, is surrounded by many warm and caring friends, as well as a large family on her husband, Todd's, side, so I didn't feel the burden as much on myself as I had in the early years of her illnesses. She has a "village" around her now.

With regard to my mother, Heidi and I are the only relatives she has any contact with, so managing caregiving for her was more challenging. Among all of the family caregivers that I've met and worked with, those with the least support have the most difficulty.

I notice myself sounding like a victim here, but I really don't feel that. I deeply believe that there is meaning and important lessons to be learned from everything that occurs in our lives. One of the many valuable lessons this time around was the importance of reaching out for support, which I did. Instead of waiting for friends, for example, to offer help, I was proactive and vulnerable with the people I was close to. I let them know how emotionally difficult this was for me, and how I really did need them, particularly for emotional support. Asking for help was hard, but I knew it was absolutely necessary. I also asked Heidi to participate in any ways that she could, and she made regular calls to my mother. Asking her was difficult, too. She had three kids and her own illnesses to contend with. But, I thought, we are family and I can at least have a discussion with her about this. She wanted to participate and was glad that I made the request.

If you are a family caregiver, it's likely that you need more support than ever before. Finding help and then explicitly asking for what you need is not always easy. The more support you can garner, though, the better off you will be. Your care recipient will also benefit from any help that you receive.

At this time, I was confronted with another one of my greatest fears: caregiving for my mother with little or no support if she was in a very difficult emotional or physical state. That was the situation when my father died in 1992, and Mom fell into a period of depression that lasted for almost three years. She cut off contact with all friends and the few remaining members of her family, other than Heidi and me. I completely shut off my own grief for a time and focused on doing whatever I could to help her remain functional and to handle financial and practical matters in her life. Memories from that time and a fear of repeating all of that haunted me for a number of days. My work was cut out for me.

I absorbed too much of Mom's emotional torment after my father's death. In her presence, I often seemed unable to maintain connection to my own strong and stable center, as I had learned to do with friends and the people I served. I was reactive to her emotional states. If she seemed calmer, or more at ease, I'd feel relaxed and hopeful. When her moods plummeted, so did mine. At times, I thought that I was of little use emotionally to either of us. I also felt completely responsible for "saving her," and was despondent over the many months of trying everything I knew to help, but to no avail. When I became simply too overwhelmed, I put my foot down and told her I couldn't keep trying to rescue her, that she'd simply have to go to a psychiatrist to get on medication, or I was going to pull way back. She went with me to an excellent geriatric psychiatrist who found the right medication for her, and her life began to turn around in wonderful ways.

This current situation triggered these memories from eighteen years earlier, and I knew that I needed to practice all that I've written about in this book.

Self-care had to be at the top of the list. I always feel relieved when I see caregivers realize the importance of self-care and am happy when they're able to have this insight in the early period of their caregiving. I needed to be emotionally, spiritually, and physically fit to respond to this situation in the healthiest possible ways for all of us. As I said, I reached out to John and many wonderful friends for help for myself. I needed perceptive people to help me process the feelings this was evoking and to help me brainstorm about how to deal with the various situations that came up.

Internal resources were just as important as were external sources of support. Soul letters proved to be invaluable. "She hasn't eaten for two days. What shall I do? What do I need for myself today so that I can fully show up for Mom? How should I work with this fear? What does Mom need most from me today? How do I deal with the differing doctors' opinions? What kind of support do I need this evening?" Just writing the letters was calming, and the answers were spot on. They revealed the wisdom that lay beneath the tangled thoughts I sometimes couldn't unhook from. I also did a lot of stream writing just to express and release the frustrations and worries that were swimming around in my psyche. My journal became a valuable ally.

Creative expression saved me once again, as I've seen it do for so many. I turned to drawing and collage quite often over the eight months and kept my commitment to these practices in spite of the fact that my mind kept telling me that I didn't have time for any "frivolous activity." I stood up to these intrusive thoughts and false notions because, after many years, I know that "art makes people sane and happy," as Julia Cameron, author of *The Artist's Way,* says. My artistic expression, simple and untrained as it is, gave me access to my imagination and to the healing effects of color and images. I get out of my head when I sit down with pens, decorative papers, scissors, glue, and magazines. My senses awaken, and the delighted child in me comes alive.

In the early weeks, my resistance was strong. Often in a state of continuously saying "no" to what was occurring, my self talk was "No. This can't be happening now. It shouldn't be happening. Tomorrow I'll call and she'll be back to her perky, busy self. There's no room for this in my life right now. I'm writing the book. I have so many projects on my plate. No! She's not that sick." Such resistance in the early phases of caregiving is common. We often aren't prepared for this life event and don't yet have strategies and resources in place for coping with all of the challenges that confront us.

My investment in things being different from what they actually were was creating a lot of suffering, both for me and for my mother. The more I was tied up in knots, resisting reality, the less I was fully present for my mother and for the variety of tasks at hand.

As I finally let go of control and relaxed my attempts to brace against "what was so," a lot changed. Facing the truth that this wasn't just a weekend event, that she had very intense and uncomfortable symptoms, and that she really was depressed, freed me to feel a deep sadness and also to get in touch with the love and empathy I had for my mother. I could also feel how difficult the whole situation was and could simply acknowledge that. Spaciousness opened up inside me and then between the two of us. Mother and daughter were meeting soul to soul.

I began doing a practice called "Hello Goodbye" to work with the concept of impermanence. I said Hello Goodbye to a frustrating conversation with a medical assistant, to too much traffic on the Golden Gate Bridge on the way to Mom's house, and to the ever-changing positive experiences, as well. Hello Goodbye to her eating a hearty dinner and Hello Goodbye to a friend fixing her TV.

It's one thing to know intellectually that all things come and go, yet another to apply that wisdom not only in the face of difficulty, but also in situations that are pleasurable and that we want to hold on to.

Being reminded of the truth of impermanence and the great relief that ensues when we accept "what is so" were some of the gifts of this challenging time. There were other rewards, as well. Acknowledging the soul gifts all along the way was very helpful in terms of keeping me from getting lost in the steady stream of problems and sinking into excessive self pity. As we saw in Chapter One—Soul Gifts, specifically identifying how we're growing, what we're learning, and what the other rewards of caregiving are is empowering and helps place this experience in a wider perspective. No longer ill-fated victims, we discover the possibilities for personal transformation that are presented to us in times of adversity.

What were the gifts? I faced something I'd always feared, and that strengthened me. Facing our fears builds confidence and makes us stronger and more resilient. I also learned how to stand up to doctors with strong opinions that were different from mine and actually convinced one of them to keep mom on a medication I thought she needed to stay on. A great esteem builder! In reaching out for advice and support early on, I strengthened my asking and receiving muscles. My mother and I developed a deeper relationship as a result of going through something very hard together and coming out on the other side. We took many risks with each other, expressing some long-buried feelings and speaking our truths, albeit uncomfortable. Our communication is better now than it's ever been. Boundaries were an issue, as well. I learned once again that I can set limits and say "no" and that the sky won't fall if I do. I was reminded of the gift of learning to surrender into not knowing. Fortunately, in our situation, my mother's health greatly improved after about eight months. I am not under any illusion that she is completely cured and won't have recurrences.

There is more...

It was the end of May 2011, about a year after the onset of my mother's symptoms. Heidi was in the fifth month of her pregnancy (yes—number four!) She found a lump in her breast and her doctor wanted her to have a biopsy. As soon as she mentioned the lump to me, I sensed danger, and was very afraid.

Phone call. "The tumor's malignant, Mom." "Oh God, not this," I thought. My world shattered into a million pieces, but I quickly composed myself to show up for my girl. "I'm so sorry, Heid. So, so sorry." I was stunned and heartbroken. I could barely speak.

Heidi was diagnosed with an aggressive form of breast cancer and had to begin the first of eight sessions of chemotherapy right away. Everything happened very fast. Her entire focus up to that point had been on her pregnancy and dealing with symptoms of A.S. and Crohn's that had recently been activated. "Cancer on top of this?" I thought. "A new baby in the middle of chemo treatments? How can we get through this one?" We all cried and talked and worried and strategized about this new development, and obsessed about how to tell my mother. I worried about whether or not she had the right doctors, how Heidi's already precarious health would fit into all of this, and how the baby would be affected. Hundreds of questions for all of us, some answers, and then just a lot of being scared, moving forward, and having to trust.

Heidi learned that she would need to have three surgeries over the coming months: repair of a fistula from the Crohn's, a double mastectomy, and removal of her ovaries. It was detected that she has the gene for hereditary breast and ovarian cancer, which is why they would remove her ovaries.

It became obvious to me from the very beginning that I would need to draw on everything I knew about self-care, and then some, so that I would be up to what was clearly going to be a long, arduous experience. I knew that my spiritual practices, including, for me, creative expression, were an absolute necessity so that I could be present and available for Heidi, Todd, and the children, and not be completely overwhelmed myself by this daunting challenge. Here was the next Everest and I needed to make a 100% commitment to being in shape for this.

I was so grateful that I had learned all that I had about caregiving. I had a large toolkit by now and knew that I'd be using everything in it. I knew the types of challenges that might lie ahead, and that I needed to avail myself of every possible resource.

"What do you need?" asked my good friend, Toni. "I don't know exactly right now, Tone," I responded. "And it's hard to turn to you, or anyone," I said. "I feel like I've outworn my welcome, especially after last year's situation with Mom." Toni assured me, as did all of my close friends, that they were there for the long haul, as I had always been for them. I shared more with them about the fears that were arising about being and needing too much, and asked them to be honest with me about their limits. They agreed to do that, and our relationships have deepened and become stronger as a result of our mutual honesty, openness, and vulnerability.

Just as my "village" showed up for me, Heidi's "village" showed up for her. Not a day went by that I didn't either see or hear about some new way that Heidi's and Todd's friends and family members were offering assistance and support. Anywhere from three to six friends were with Heidi for every chemo treatment and five friends were there for the birth. People provided dinners for the whole family every day throughout the treatments, and she was showered with gifts: scarves, slippers, hats, books, CDs, and presents for the baby. Every month an anonymous person left a big box of either apples or oranges on their front porch. A team came in and re-organized part of the house to get ready for the new baby. My wish when we found out that Heidi had breast cancer was that she be gently and lovingly carried through this both by her strong faith and strength, and by whoever and whatever the universe would provide for support. My wish was granted a thousand times over, and my gratitude for this is as big as the sky.

This outpouring of love and generosity has made me even more sensitive to the care receivers and their families who don't have this kind of unflagging support. I think about this often and feel very sad about it. I have met and worked with many caregivers who desperately needed much more support than they had. I know that one of the reasons that I've been able to weather this storm as well as I have is that I have not been holding it alone.

From the first moments of this journey, I sensed that a huge transformation was about to occur in my life. I had the image of layers of my old self being stripped away, a dismantling of my former identity. I also sensed that I needed to deeply surrender to this whole process, that life was presenting me with something that was going to be big, harrowing, and wholly unpredictable.

And so it has been, and continues to be. In addition to Heidi's experience with cancer, we have a new child, Sarah, in the family, who is healthy and thriving. I have really learned how to live in the present and in "the mystery." Much of the time now I am able to just be with the many large and small questions that arise every day. I am saying "Yes" to most everything now: a big "Yes" to the constant twists and turns of life, to living with uncertainty, to confusion, clarity, frustration, ease, powerlessness, strength, and so much more. I make room for fear, grief, anger, and every other feeling that this triggers. I don't want to run from the inevitable pain that is part and parcel of this great challenge. To me, showing up fully means that I have access to and can express all of my human qualities as well as the transcendent dimensions of my nature. I am saying "Yes" to my humanness and "Yes" to my divine nature. For we are all of it: finite and infinite, immanent and transcendent, spirit and matter. There really is no separation.

Joy and celebration were not absent from this difficult experience. Heidi let Sam throw Nerf darts at her bald head and Sophie, wanting to look like Mom, had a fashion show with Heidi's scarves. Sarah has delighted everyone and Sadie continues to remind all of us what it's like to love, relax, and live in the moment.

I am grateful, and it's a bittersweet gratitude, to have had the opportunity to once again apply and test many of the principles and practices that comprise *Soul Care for Caregivers* and to offer it to you even more wholeheartedly that I could have before. Hello Goodbye.

Appendix One

ADDITIONAL GUIDELINES FOR RESILIENCE AND SELF-CARE

Here are some more tips and tools to aid you on your caregiver's journey:

Learn about your care recipient's illness. This applies primarily to informal caregivers since caregiving professionals are knowledgeable about the illnesses they are treating. There are vast resources on the web and many disease-specific sites that will provide you with information, research, other links, and a variety of additional resources. There are also more general sites, like www.webmd.com, www.healthcentral.com, and www.medscape. com that provide useful information. (See Appendix Three—Resources for Information and Support.) In addition, you can ask your care recipient's health care providers to give you brochures and suggest other relevant sources for information. Becoming knowledgeable about symptoms, the etiology of the disease, typical progressions of the disease, treatments, what to expect before, during, and after treatments, medications, side effects of medications, and other pertinent information is beneficial for you, the care receiver, and others involved in the caregiving.

Identify the support services and community resources for care receivers and caregivers that may be available to you. Possibilities are: home health care organizations, social service agencies, adult day care centers, respite care, hospice programs, transportation services, educational programs, caregiver support groups, caregiver training programs, local disease-specific organizations that provide education and support for caregivers, counselors, spiritual counselors, and the volunteer services that are provided by many churches, synagogues, and mosques.

Practice asking for help. This is challenging for many of us who are caregivers. It stretches us beyond our comfort zone. We see ourselves as the helpers, and we may feel as if we're weak, not resourceful enough, lazy, or, perhaps, irresponsible if we ask for help. We're not used to doing this. If this is difficult for you, take small steps in order to build your "asking for help" muscle. Practice in safe places in your life, for example, with good friends or trusted family members, initially requesting a small favor, such as picking up a book that you ordered at the bookstore that you know is on their way home. Once you are comfortable with this new behavior, gradually stretch yourself even more, and ask for a friend to give you a back rub or water your plants when you're away from home. Moving outside of our comfort zones naturally stimulates fear and anxiety. We stay with the known and familiar in order to avoid the experience of anxiety. Don't wait for fear to disappear before you act. My mother has this quote on her bedroom mirror "Do what you fear. Watch it disappear."

Vary what you do and how you perform tasks and duties. If you notice yourself becoming bored or frustrated by repetitious routines, such as preparing and serving the same or very similar meals day after day, bring variation to mealtime. Put flowers on the bed tray. Add something colorful to the plate, or play music during meals. During lunch, read a book aloud that both of you would enjoy. If you bring your creativity to everyday activities, you will feel more alive, and your recipient will receive the benefits not only of some new and different things going on in their environment, but also of your being invigorated by tapping into your own creativity. "Variety is the spice of life."

Look for ways to encourage autonomy and independence in your care receiver. Most care recipients want to feel more empowered and are despondent, sometimes angry, about their diminished capacity to care for themselves. They may be unable or unwilling to communicate this clearly. Watch out for the tendency to overdo your helping, to be the caregiver who "cares too much." In an attempt to be the best caregivers they can be, that is, responsible, thorough, generous, and helpful in every way, caregivers can, at times, provide more care than is actually needed, doing things for the care recipient that they could do for themselves. They will also at times do things themselves because it is quicker and easier. Each day, carefully assess what you truly need to do, knowing that is likely to change based on the recipient's condition and numerous other external factors. Look for ways to foster independence in the person in your care; for example, offer the possibility of participating in choices and decisions, helping with simple tasks, such as folding laundry or assisting with the preparation of meals. Caring for something or someone is life-affirming and empowering. Give your care receiver something that requires care and attention, such as a houseplant or even a pet. Giving care to another is life-giving in itself.

Maintain your connections to others and to the "outside world." Many caregivers, particularly family and friend caregivers who are doing long-term caregiving, become isolated. The tasks and duties may be all consuming, especially if there's a lack of support from others. Caregiving can be a lonely job. Often, there seem to be too few hours in a day. You may be tired, sometimes overwhelmed. As stress mounts, some caregivers start shutting down and cutting themselves off from others. Maintaining friendships and other connections outside of the caregiving arena can seem like just one more thing to do, yet another item to add to the never-ending list. Isolation can be a breeding ground for loneliness, apathy, and depression. This is a common and sometimes serious problem for family/friend caregivers. Of course, some withdrawal is natural and necessary. Caregiving involves so much giving and sharing of ourselves. We expend a lot of time and energy, and caregiving is a one-way street at times, with little coming back. Going inward is natural and necessary. There is a difference, though, between healthy reflective solitude and cutting yourself off from others. Connecting with others, even for short periods, can be sustaining. Contact with people who are caring and supportive can enhance your energy and well-being rather than further deplete you.

Learn practices for centering and managing stress. (See Chapter Two—Boulders on the Path.) We all have different ways of finding balance, calming ourselves, and managing stress. I'm a strong believer in doing what works for you rather than following someone else's prescription. A problem for many people is that there are too many options for wellness practices and they don't know how or what to choose. Some of these include breathing processes, relaxation techniques, meditation, prayer, guided imagery, yoga, tai chi or qi gong, swimming, running, biking, and hiking, to name just a few. I've known many people, especially living in California as I do, who feel guilty because they don't have a traditional form of meditation practice. One size simply does not fit all. Knitting, listening to music, looking outside the window at trees and birds, painting, writing, gardening, or cooking can have the same balancing and centering effects as a sitting meditation practice. Also, all of these practices, including meditation, writing, and gardening, are tools that can help us "unhook" from our busy minds and connect with our true nature. They help to free us from our limited and constricted mental constructs and open us to the wider field of being. When I write, at times the sense of a separate self drops away, and I feel a part of something much greater than myself.

Writing is definitely one of my practices. When I relax, let go, and write from a place of openness and presence, with my attention off of results, I move from the surface of my psyche to my deep interior. I move into the spaces between words, my breathing naturally deepens, senses become more alive, and pockets of feeling open wide to be held in the larger field of Being. The same is true for when I "officially" meditate. I'm reminded of a talk on meditation that I attended many years ago. The presenter asked a woman in the first row who had been asking astute and perceptive questions what her practice was. "I knit," she answered.

Finding time for self-care practices is difficult for most caregivers, but don't let the fact that you don't have long blocks of time for self-care keep you from doing things that can fortify and revitalize you. Perhaps going to the seashore and listening to the waves is one of your favorite centering activities, but your caregiving duties don't afford you the time to go there. If you can't get to the ocean, take five to ten minutes with your eyes closed and vividly imagine yourself lying on the beach, feeling the warmth of the sun against your skin, relaxing from your head to your toes as you enjoy the rhythmic sounds of the waves. If you include all of your senses when you practice self-guided imagery, you are more likely to achieve your desired results. Of course, it's not the same as actually being there, but the imagination is very powerful and can alter your emotional and physiological states even when practiced for short periods.

Exercise and good nutrition are important. Whenever I see suggestions to exercise and eat well, I tend to skip over that advice because everyone says it and everyone knows it. Even though I know it and recommend it to others, as well, I don't find it easy to maintain a regular exercise schedule or to always eat what's good for me. I don't have any easy answers here. I just know that when I walk at least five times a week, I'm more energetic, alive, calm, present, and even happier. I am more limber. Pains recede. There is research on the health benefits of regular exercise, and I see these benefits in my own experience and that of the many people I know who include exercise in their wellness regimes. You'll feel better and have more stamina if you exercise regularly, or even sometimes. But don't let your Inner Critic berate you if you don't.

Food: a great pleasure and formidable challenge for many people. As we all know, sugar, chocolate, coffee, bread, and all those yummy foods we love to eat in restaurants or while we're watching TV can be as addictive as alcohol or cigarettes. I became a more mindful eater not because I had great self control and was so committed to healthy living, but simply because I started becoming more and more sensitive to the negative effects of some of these addictive foods, in my case, sugar and wheat. Isn't that in everything that tastes good, you ask? Well, yes. But the sugar blues and uncomfortable symptoms of a wheat allergy started to become debilitating, and I no longer felt I had a choice. I actually see myself as fortunate in this regard. Without these symptoms, I'd probably be lusting after chocolate chip cookies or wolfing down a pint of Cherry Garcia a few times a week. Since I've decreased my consumption of these foods, I have more vitality and look and feel healthier than ever. I try to avoid becoming preachy about this to others because I know how hard the food struggle can be and I know that you can only do what you can do when you are ready to do it.

Keep well-being reminders where you'll see them. You can create a Well-Being Poster, for example, with pictures, words, and phrases that represent well-being to you. Add to it whenever you'd like. Post-its are great for reminders, too, for example, Pause, Breathe, Let Go, Return to the Present, Keep It Simple, Laugh, Be Silly, Be Here Now, Risk, and any other words, phrases, or slogans that help you remember what is important to you. Also, images are very powerful. Reflecting on an image for even a short time can help you access your imagination, your feeling nature, and your spirit. Go through some magazines and choose images that you associate with well-being. Put some of those pictures up in your living and work space, and pause to take them in from time to time. "A picture is worth a thousand words."

Remember why you want to be in the helping role. Many of you would not have chosen to be doing this. Caregiving may have been thrust upon you because no one else in the family or your circle of friends was willing or available to fulfill this role. Perhaps you do want to be a caregiver because you care so much about the person you are helping. If you are a volunteer or health care professional, you chose this work for many reasons. You wanted to help alleviate suffering, to make a difference in the world, to give back, to share your heart and soul with others.

Remembering why you want to be a caregiver can reconnect you with your highest motivations and intentions. It can also help in those times when the challenges seem overwhelming and you just want to turn around and run away.

Take action on insights. If you have a realization, for example, that taking your paints and brushes out of the closet and beginning to paint again might be the best thing you could do for yourself or you have the insight that calling your sister to deal with the impasse you've been experiencing with her for weeks would free something up in you, it helps to take even a small step right away. Either pick up the phone, or go to your calendar and choose a date and time to call her. Take out those painting materials, and clear a space to begin as soon as possible. Commitment and follow-through on insights is a great esteem builder. Just take that first step. Once you do, the next steps get easier and easier.

Think small. I'm a great believer in baby steps with regard to the achievement of any goal. Many people believe that big leaps are the only way to make big changes. You can achieve any goal, for example, become more organized or follow through on projects, by creating small, attainable goals. How does this work? When you establish small goals and follow through on them, your psyche receives a new message from you, that is, you become someone who means what you say. You believe yourself.

What I've seen happen so often is that we start out with wonderful intentions for a project; then, for a variety of different reasons, don't follow through with our plans or complete the project. Then we end up feeling bad about ourselves. If this happens more than occasionally, we lose confidence in our ability to stay with or complete projects and then sometimes lose the motivation to even try to establish any more goals or plans. This is a painful cycle. Baby steps are a good way to break this cycle.

When you take baby steps, which can be as tiny as "for two minutes every day this week, I will….," you are building a solid internal foundation of accomplishments slowly but surely. This increases your confidence and prepares the ground for the bigger goals you are leading up to. After a week of spending two minutes a day on your project, then five minutes a day the following week, it's likely that you will follow through on your intention to spend an hour or two hours a day on it because you've been following through on your intentions for perhaps six weeks. It works!

Remember to laugh. Humor helps us cope. It relieves tension and provides you with opportunities for freshness and aliveness. Laughter is good medicine—some say the best medicine!

Appendix Two

LEARN HOW TO DISARM THE INNER CRITIC

As a caregiver, if you believe your inner critic when it is attacking you with its caustic commentary, you will feel inadequate, not good enough, incompetent, selfish, lazy, and irresponsible, to name a few things. The critic is a voice within us that we mistakenly identify with and believe. It is an internalization of criticisms and expectations that have been imposed on us by others and blaming, judging, and shaming messages that have been directed at us for much of our lives. From the perspective of the inner critic, we are never enough. We must be more and do more. We must always act appropriately and never make mistakes. We must be perfect and always do our jobs perfectly. The inner critic is never satisfied.

The wonderful news is that YOU ARE NOT YOUR INNER CRITIC. It is a voice within you, and you can be free of its oppressive influence in your life. Here are some tips for disarming the inner critic. It helps to have an inner critic Toolkit, a variety of strategies to use at different times.

1. Get to know your inner critic and recognize when it is present. Write down the critical thoughts. See if the voice is male or female. Notice when and how it shows up with regard to your caregiving. Ask yourself if the messages remind you of anyone from your past. A parent? Both parents? Siblings? Teachers or religious leaders? Peers? Discover what situations activate the critic more than others. Is your self-judgment stronger when you're tired, stressed, or not feeling well? Look for patterns and how to identify his/her voice.

2. Identify underlying feelings. When you experience a "critic attack," stop and let yourself experience the feelings that may underlie the judging voice. Perhaps you're afraid of rejection or loss. Relax into the feeling, allowing fear, for example, to simply be present. Acknowledge this part of you that is afraid. The critic often quiets down when we tap into the deeper layers of feeling that reside at its core.

3. Shift your attention. Move. Engage in a different activity. Focus on something that is absorbing.

4. Take a stand. At times, being assertive will disarm the critic. Be firm, talk back, and tell the inner critic to "Stop! Now!"

5. When you silence the critic's commentary, direct your awareness to the voice of your soul—the calm, wise knowing within you. Ask your inner wisdom what it wants to express to you or, perhaps, pose questions like: What is right action for me now? What will help me get centered and clear again?

6. Reach out for support. Rather than imploding when you're in the throes of self-judgment and getting more deeply mired in negativity, contact a trusted friend. Talk to someone who is empathetic and can listen to you with loving care and attention. At times, just speaking about your discomfort will defuse it.

Be patient in this process of liberating yourself from the critic within. It took many years for this pattern to develop in your psyche, and it will take time to disentangle from it. Let this be the imperfect process that it is with steps forward and some steps back. And try not to judge yourself for having a tenacious inner critic!

Appendix Three

RESOURCES FOR INFORMATION AND SUPPORT

Websites for Caregiver Information and Support

www.aarp.org/caregiving
  The website for American Association for Retired Persons—tip sheets, articles, and interactive features

www.caregiver.com
  Today's Caregiver magazine for family and professional caregivers—articles, advice, interviews with caregivers, online support groups, free e-newsletter

www.caregiver.org
  The website for The Family Caregiver Alliance—education, services, research, and advocacy

www.caregiving.org

A coalition of grassroots organizations, professional associations, service organizations, disease-specific organizations, a government agency, and corporations that focus on issues related to caregiving

www.caregiverrelieffund.org

A social venture committed to caring for caregivers— resources, assistance, and a voice for caregivers

www.caregiverslibrary.org

An online library for caregivers

www.extension.org

The website for Extension Family Caregiving—articles and online learning activities

www.nfcacares.org

The website for the National Family Caregivers' Association—tips and tools, quarterly newsletter, educational materials, and information on agencies and organizations that provide caregiver support

www.strengthforcaring.com

Information about health conditions, caregiving stories, tips for stress relief, resources for creating community with other caregivers

www.thefamilycaregiver.org

Education, support, and advocacy

Organizations for Caregivers

Administration on Aging (www.aoa.gov)

330 Independence Avenue SW, Washington, DC 20201

American Medical Association (www.ama-assn.org)
515 North State Street, Chicago, IL 60610

American Red Cross (www.redcross.org)
2025 E Street NW, Suite SE 1068, Washington, DC 20006

Assisted Living Federation of America (www.alfa.org)
1650 King Street, Suite 602, Alexandria, VA 22314-2747

Department of Veteran Affairs (www.va.gov)
810 Vermont Avenue NW, Washington, DC 20420

Hospice Foundation of America (www.hospicefounda-tion.org)
2001S. Street NW #300, Washington, DC 20009

National Hospice and Palliative Care Organization (www.nhpco.org)
1700 Diagonal Road, Arlington, VA 22314

National Institute of Health (www.nih.gov)
9000 Rockville Pike, Bethesda, Maryland 20894

US Department of Health and Human Services (www.hhs.gov)
200 Independence Avenue SW, Washington, DC 20201

Acknowledgments

First and foremost, I wish to thank the many family and professional caregivers who shared their struggles and their successes with me. I marvel at your courage and dedication.

I am deeply grateful to my daughter, Heidi Virkus, who has been an inspiration to me throughout her life for the way she has met life's challenges. You have used everything to further your growth and, then, turned around to share what you've learned with others, including me. I'm a very lucky mom! I am so grateful to Todd Virkus for supporting Heidi in "all the right ways" and for being the best dad ever to my cherished grandchildren.

Heartfelt appreciation goes to my mother, Jacquie Friedman, who believed in this book from the very beginning. Her resolute and steady support of my brother every day of his life modeled what is possible for me in my own caregiving.

I want to express deep gratitude to my husband, John, for his editorial wizardry and for always having the patience of a saint with me. You are a mensch.

Many thanks to the Lloyd Symington Foundation for its enthusiastic support of my work and for providing the grant that allowed me to turn my vision into reality.

The generosity and wisdom of my wonderful friends provided a strong foundation that carried me through the ups and downs of developing and writing this book. Hugs and thanks to: Toni and Philip Brooks, Hillary Davis, Ted Strauss, Jennifer Mayol, Michael Grossman, Roberta Heath Bradshaw, Whitt Bradshaw, Deborah Boyar, Terry Patten, Saniel Bonder, Linda Groves-Bonder, Debbie Ford, David Coates, Sandra Glickman, Michael Schwartz, Daniel Ellenberg, Judith Bell, Marilyn Gordon, Elizabeth Ferguson, Raphael Angeles, Michael Archer, Darlene and Lawrence Martin, Susan and Dave Albers, Philippe Berthoud, Peter Drake, Toby Symington, Chellsa Avelin, David Lesser, Karen Pando-Mars, Susan Mall, Junelle Porter, Bonita Zola Williams, Rene Jewel Hansen, Laura Elliott, Dave Pleasants, Inder Bhoghal, Rain Stickney, Shoshana Rosenfeld, Brooks Toll, Ardith Dean, and Anita Fisk.

Thank you to Javy Galindo and your superb editorial staff for your sound advice and insightful feedback. Many thanks, also, to Xavi Callahan for your expertise and encouragement in the important initial phases of the book's development.

I'm grateful to the members of my *Writing from the Soul* groups who, by example, ever-remind me to practice what I teach.

I want to acknowledge my colleagues, students, and the staff at John F. Kennedy University where I have worked since 1986. Special appreciation to Janis McKinstry, Terri Davis, Chuck Burack, Daramola Cabral, Bill Garrett, Cyd Jenefsky, Michael G. Mulholland, Charlene Tuckerson, Jessica Newberry, Anne Marie Taylor, Ray Greenleaf, Marilyn Fowler, and Vernice Solimar.

Big thanks to the Waking Down in Mutuality community for their wisdom and dedicated support. I also want to acknowledge the Psychosynthesis community for giving me my foundation in psychospiritual principles and practices.

Finally, much gratitude to Human Sun Media for their enthusiasm about the book and belief in me and my work.

About the Author

Susanne West, MA, CPC, CHT, is a Professor of Psychology at John F. Kennedy University. She teaches in the B.A. Psychology and B.A. Health Sciences Programs in the College of Undergraduate Studies and the Integral Psychology, Consciousness and Transformative Studies, and Holistic Health Programs in the College of Graduate and Professional Studies. Susanne is the recipient of the Harry L. Morrison Distinguished Teaching Award at JFKU. She is also on the faculty of the Center for Hypnotherapy, where she has developed and teaches guided imagery certification programs.

Susanne is a life coach and integrative spiritual teacher who works with individuals and groups. She also facilitates Soul Care for Caregivers groups and workshops, Writing from the Soul, and Creativity and Awakening groups, workshops, and teleseminars. In addition, she is on the teaching staff of Waking Down in Mutuality.

Visit Susanne's website: www.susannewest.com

Made in the USA
Middletown, DE
22 June 2019